BETTE DAVIS

The Pictorial Treasury of Film Stars

BETTE DAVIS

by
JERRY VERMILYE

General Editor: **TED SENNETT**

GALAHAD BOOKS · NEW YORK CITY

For
Franklyn Lenthall—
who knows what actors
are all about

This Galahad Books edition is published by
arrangement with Pyramid Communications, Inc.

Copyright ©1973 by Pyramid Communications, Inc.

ISBN 0-88365-167-X

Library of Congress Catalog Card Number: 73-90220

Printed in the United States of America

PREFACE

By TED SENNETT

"The movies!" Flickering lights in the darkness that stirred our imaginations and haunted our dreams. All of us cherish memories of "going to the movies" to gasp at feats of derring-do, to roar with laughter at clownish antics, to weep at acts of noble sacrifice. For many filmgoers, the events on the screen were not only larger than life but also more mysterious, more fascinating, and—when times were bad—more rewarding. And if audiences could be blamed for preferring movies to life, they never seemed to notice, or care.

Of course the movies have always been more than a source of wish-fulfillment or a repository for nostalgic memories. From the first unsteady images to today's most experimental efforts, motion pictures have mirrored America's social history, and over the decades they have developed into an internationally esteemed art.

As social history, movies reflect our changing tastes, styles, and ideas. To our amusement, they show us how we looked and behaved: flappers with bobbed hair and bee-stung lips cavorting at "wild" parties; gangsters and G-men in striped suits and wide-brimmed hats exchanging gunfire in city streets; pompadoured "swing-shift" Susies and dashing servicemen, "working for Uncle Sam." To our chagrin, they show us the innocent (and sometimes not so innocent) lies we believed: that love triumphs over all adversity and even comes to broad-shouldered lady executives; that war is an heroic and virtually bloodless activity; that fame and success can be achieved indiscriminately by chorus girls, scientists, football players, and artists. To our edification, they show us how we felt about marriage in the twenties, crime in the thirties, war in the forties, big business in the fifties, and youth in the sixties. (Presumably future filmgoers will know how we felt about sex in the seventies.)

As an influential art, motion pictures are being studied and analyzed as never before by young filmgoers who are excited by the medium's past accomplishments and its even greater potential for the future. The rich body of films from *Intolerance* to *The Godfather;* the work of directors from Griffith to Kubrick; the uses of film for documenting events, ideas, and even emotions—these are the abundant materials from which film courses and film societies are being created across the country.

THE PICTORIAL TREASURY OF FILM STARS also draws on these materials, encompassing in a series of publications all the people, the trends, and the concepts that have contributed to motion pictures as nostalgia, as social history, and as art. The books in the series range as widely as the camera-eye can take us, from the distant past when artists with a vision of film's possibilities shaped a new form of expression, to the immediate future, when the medium may well undergo changes as innovative as the first primitive movements.

THE PICTORIAL TREASURY OF FILM STARS is a tribute to achievement: to the charismatic stars who linger in all our memories, and to the gifted people behind the cameras: the directors, the producers, the writers, the editors, the cameramen. It is also a salute to everyone who loves movies, forgives their failures, and acknowledges their shortcomings, who attends Bogart and Marx Brothers revivals and Ingmar Bergman retrospectives and festivals of forthcoming American and European films.

"The movies!" The cameras turn and the flickering images begin. And again we settle back to watch the screen, hoping to see a dream made real, an idea made palpable, or a promise fulfilled. On that unquenchable hope alone, the movies will endure.

CONTENTS

ACKNOWLEDGMENTS

Little, Brown & Co., Publishers; The Memory Shop, New York; Kenneth G. Lawrence and the Movie Memorabilia Shop of Hollywood; Ted Sennett, my editor, for his valued aid and inspiration.

Quotations from *The Lonely Life*, by Bette Davis, are reprinted by permission of G. P. Putnam's Sons, copyright (c) 1962 by Bette Davis.

INTRODUCTION

Mimics and impersonators have owed entire careers to Bette Davis. Her famous bug-eyes, disdainful slash of a mouth, and distinctive pelvic walk are easily imitated. Her ambulatory elbows and wet-nail-polish gestures, her omnipresent cigarettes and clipped speech patterns, with their occasional oddball line-readings, have been aped for many years.

The outward sound and look are ripe for imitation; the inner Bette Davis is not. It is this inner person—the enduring, charismatic professional actress who survived all the mannerisms —we will consider in this book.

On reflection, Bette Davis would seem as unlikely a film star as ever reached stardom. Beauty didn't get her there. Ability did, but talent was not enough. Her long career bears the battle scars of continuing fights with studio heads to get decent roles in worthwhile films with literate scripts and competent craftsmen, both before and behind the cameras.

She has survived because she comes from solid New England stock, and Yankees are tough. Her rugged constitution took her from an itinerant childhood, through a fatherless adolescence, and countless schools. And after proving her acting ability on New York stages, Davis had the courage to crash Hollywood in the early years of talking pictures, when glamour and physical beauty were prerequisites for female stardom. Davis had neither. Some of her early employers wondered why they had hired such an ugly duckling: "She has as much sex appeal as Slim Summerville!" remarked Universal's Carl Laemmle, Jr.

She has survived because of the rare quality that keeps the viewer mesmerized by her performances and fascinated to learn what she will do next, and how she'll do it, even when her material is less than superb. Through sheer force of personality she can make you think she's beautiful, make you weep for her, make you loathe her. As an actress she has courageously run the gamut of roles and genres, often with great success. Other times she has failed. Charles Laughton once told her, "Never stop daring to hang yourself, Bette!" And she has heeded his advice over the years.

She has survived because she is a thoroughbred original who flourished in a Hollywood lotusland of studio acting-stables that have become only a memory.

Bette Davis. Professional actress. And, in the very special sense of the word, a star.

Prophetically, she was born in the middle of an electrical storm on April 5, 1908, in the Boston-area industrial city of Lowell, Massachusetts. They named her Ruth Elizabeth. Her father, Harlow Morrell Davis, was an independent-minded, humorless patent attorney of Welsh-English heritage. His wife, the former Ruth Favor, was descended from a French Huguenot family. Eighteen months after the birth of Ruth Elizabeth the Davises welcomed another child, Barbara. To the two young Davis girls their stern father was "Daddy," but their mother they called "Ruthie," a name reflecting their lifelong emotional proximity.

In 1915, after the Davises were divorced, Ruthie and her two daughters moved to Newton. Ruthie accepted a position as governess in New York City, and the girls were sent to Crestalban, a farm school in the Berkshires. It was there that young Ruth Elizabeth first experienced the power of holding an audience. One Christmas, dressed as Santa Claus, she brushed against a candle-lit tree and her costume caught fire. Her rescuers beat out the flames by wrapping her in a rug. When they took the rug away, the child decided to make believe she had been blinded.

ORIGINS: MASSACHUSETTS TO BROADWAY (1908-1930)

The ruse worked. Says Davis, "A shudder of delight went through me. I was in complete command of the moment. I had never known such power."

Long an amateur photographer, Ruthie now decided to make a profession of it. She enrolled in a New York school of photography and moved her daughters from the Berkshires to Manhattan. It was at this time that Ruth Elizabeth officially became known as "Bette" (pronounced Betty). The unique spelling derived from Balzac's novel *La Cousine Bette*—a suggestion of her mother's best friend, Myrtis Genthner.

After living in East Orange, New Jersey for a time, the Davises returned to Newton, where teen-aged Bette attended high school and led a popular social life. After an unhappy period at Northfield Seminary the girls were transferred to Cushing Academy, a coeducational school in Ashburnham, Massachusetts. There Bette waited on tables to help supplement her education and studied "Expression" with Lois Cann, according to Davis,

Determined at 12 (1920).

"a truly remarkable dramatic coach to find in a small New England school." At Cushing Bette played Lola Pratt in Booth Tarkington's *Seventeen*, in which her beau Harmon (Ham) Nelson had a character role. Years later, after many separations, they would be married.

During a summer spent at Peterboro, New Hampshire, Ruthie set up a photography studio and Bette studied at Mariarden, a school of dance and drama on the outskirts of town. Here her greatest influence was an Englishwoman with the exotic professional name of Roshanara. Under her expert tutelage Bette was cast in a professional outdoor production of Shakespeare's *A Midsummer Night's Dream*, directed by veteran actor Frank Conroy, who also played Bottom. On another occasion she danced the title role in *The Moth*, which so impressed Conroy that he told Ruthie, "You must see to it your daughter goes on the stage. She belongs there. She has something which comes across the footlights."

Following her graduation from Cushing Academy, Bette found herself at loose ends, with no money for college and no real skills. She tried to get an acting job at the Ogunquit Playhouse in Maine but was rejected as too young and inexperienced. For a while she did secretarial work for a local author, and then Ruthie took her daughters to Boston to a performance of Ibsen's *The Wild Duck*, with Blanche Yurka and Peg Entwhistle. Bette was thrilled and fascinated, and she longed to play the title role of Hedvig. She was certain of one thing—she would become a professional actress.

Fully supporting her daughter's determination, Ruthie accompanied Bette to New York in September 1928. Their mission: an interview with Eva Le Gallienne, who they hoped would accept Bette as a student at her Civic Repertory Theatre on Fourteenth Street, where the actress maintained a low-priced showcase for the classics. The interview did not go well. Asked to read the part of an elderly woman, Bette, ill at ease and somewhat irritated, responded with "That is why I want to come to your school, to learn how to play a part like this." A week later Bette was notified by letter that her attitude did not reflect a serious enough approach to theatre to warrant her being accepted at the Civic Repertory.

Undaunted, Ruthie next laid siege to the Robert Milton-John

Murray Anderson School of the Theatre. Marching Bette into the office of manager Hugh Anderson, she announced, "My daughter Bette wants to be an actress. I haven't the money for her tuition, but will assure you that you will eventually have it. Will you accept her as a student?" Nonplussed, Anderson accepted Bette.

As a drama student Bette had as her dancing instructress the famed Martha Graham, who taught the proper use of one's body on a stage. Bette worshiped her, and believes she owes all of her powers of bodily expression directly to Miss Graham. She did well at the school and was determined to win one of the two five-hundred-dollar scholarships awarded to a boy and girl each year. Her acting vehicle was the leading role in *The Famous Mrs. Fair*, played on Broadway by Margalo Gilmore. And she won.

The award was gratifying, but her acting career was making little progress. She left school for the opportunity to take a leading role in a production of *The Earth Between* at the Provincetown Playhouse in Greenwich Village, but the play was postponed. Through Frank Conroy, she got to meet George Cukor, later the leading Hollywood

director, who owned and operated a stock company in Rochester, New York. She was given a small role in his production of *Broadway* but went on to play the female lead when, in true Hollywood fashion, the actress in the role sprained her ankle. Cukor was impressed enough to engage her as ingenue for the following season. That summer Bette joined the Cape Playhouse in Dennis, Massachusetts—but as an usher.

Finally her opportunity arrived. Laura Hope Crews, who was starring in and directing *Mr. Pim Passes By*, demanded that the Playhouse management produce an ingenue who could be acceptable as an English girl. The producer submitted usher Bette Davis, whom Miss Crews accepted on the condition that she be able to sing and play on the piano an English ballad called "I Passed by Your Window." Bette got the part and scored a great personal success on opening night. She won an ovation and an offer to return the next summer as company ingenue.

That fall of 1928 Bette and her mother drove to Rochester to fulfill her season contract with George Cukor's stock company. She joined a company whose permanent members included

Frank McHugh, Wallace Ford, and Benny Baker. It was the summer players' first winter season there, and a different play was performed each week with such guest artists as Miriam Hopkins, Elizabeth Patterson, and Louis Calhern.

The company's new ingenue found it difficult to take direction. When Cukor criticized her, she would always have a comeback, an alibi for her action or behavior. It was difficult to admit she might be wrong. Finally, she was assigned to play Louis Calhern's mistress in *Yellow*, and when he complained that she looked more like his daughter, she was fired. Davis claims Cukor never gave her the reason.

However, the timing was excellent; The Provincetown Playhouse production of *The Earth Between* was now ready to proceed, and Bette signed a run-of-the-play contract for thirty-five dollars a week. But then she began to get frightened; this was a New York opening in a theater that had helped launch the careers of Katharine Cornell, Paul Robeson, and Ann Harding. Virgil Geddes' two act drama *The Earth Between* opened on March 5, 1929, preceded by Eugene O'Neill's morbid monologue, *Before Breakfast*. In *The Earth Between* Bette played the innocent sixteen-year-old daughter of a Nebraska farmer. The play bore heavy influences of O'Neill —and more than a hint of incest, although Davis admits she was too naïve at the time to fully appreciate that fact. The opening was a triumph. In *The New York Times*, Brooks Atkinson was enthusiastic: "Miss Bette Davis, who is making her first appearance, is an entrancing creature who plays in a soft, unassertive style." The other leading critic, St. John Ervine of the *World*, disliked the entire evening, although he called the plays "remarkably acted, especially by Miss Bette Davis." Davis called the opening of *The Earth Between* the most exciting event in her life. "Nothing," she says, "will ever equal the emotions I knew that night. I was a success in my first New York play!"

Bette's performance led to her being engaged to play Hedvig on tour with Blanche Yurka in *The Wild Duck*, as well as Boletta in another Ibsen play, *The Lady from the Sea*. Joining the company as a replacement for Linda Watkins, Bette Davis then made her official Broadway debut in *The Lady From the Sea*, just prior to the tour. It went off smoothly, and *The Wild Duck*

BROKEN DISHES (1929). With Donald Meek

was a great success for her. The tour proved an invaluable training ground; audiences varied, but for the young actress it was an intense nonstop love affair. Audiences were *noticing* her. In Boston, Blanche Yurka brought Bette on to share a bow, then left her alone to receive an ovation.

Following another summer at the Cape Playhouse, Davis obtained the important ingenue part in Martin Flavin's comedy *Broken Dishes*, starring Donald Meek. It opened on Broadway on November 5, 1929, at the Ritz Theatre and ran for 178 performances. The critics were quite impressed with Bette Davis's performance as a spirited girl who joins her henpecked father (Meek) in rebelling against his overbearing wife. She was now a full-fledged Broadway actress in a hit play. "I loved playing Elaine," Davis reports, "and Mr. Meek was an angel to work with." Her salary: seventy-five dollars a week. It was doubled three months later.

One night Arthur Hornblow, Jr., saw her performance in *Broken Dishes* and set up a screen test for a role in Samuel Goldwyn's *The Devil to Pay*. The test was made at Paramount's studios in Astoria. At the time Davis disliked being photographed almost as much as Goldwyn disliked her test; he is variously reported to have reacted with "Who did this to me?" "Who wasted my time with that one?" and/or "Where did you find that horrible-looking creature?" Whatever his comment, Davis agrees it was a dreadful test, with no thought given to lighting, make-up, or dress. Goldwyn quickly assigned the role to Myrna Loy.

After *Broken Dishes* closed in the spring of 1930, Bette Davis returned to Dennis for her third season of stock and then joined Meek and the *Broken Dishes* cast for a road tour. While on tour she answered an emergency call to return to New York and replace the ingenue in an incoming production, *Solid South*, with Richard Bennett. This was ten days before its Broadway opening, and Davis knew that Bennett, father of Joan and Constance, had a reputation for temperament. But she felt that the play was good and she loved her role. Despite Rouben Mamoulian's direction, and a strong cast that included Elizabeth Patterson and Jessie Royce Landis, the notices were poor, and *Solid South* lasted for only thirty-one performances.

Solid South led to Davis's second screen test, this time for

Universal Pictures. Talent scout David Werner thought she might be right for the leading lady in the film version of Preston Sturges's play *Strictly Dishonorable*, which Universal had bought. This time, she took care with her dress and make-up, and was offered three hundred dollars per week with three-month options the first year—in the event that a test of her *legs* passed muster. A week later she signed for the movies. Had she known what lay immediately ahead, says Davis, she never would have crossed the Rockies.

David Werner had told Bette Davis point-blank that she lacked the glamour and sex appeal that could guarantee screen success. But he assured her that the intensity that made people watch her on the stage could, if captured on film, make her a star. Werner said he had a hunch she would "go a long way in Hollywood." The studio then attempted to give her a name with more "appeal." Universal's publicity men thought "Bette Davis" sounded like a name for a stenographer; instead, they suggested "Bettina Dawes." Davis refused adamantly; she wouldn't have the public calling her "Between the drawers!"

In December 1930, Bette and Ruthie arrived at Los Angeles' Union Station to find no Universal representative awaiting them. As it developed, a studio man was there but reported he had seen no one who looked like an actress. Davis reports it was the appropriate beginning of a miserable year. First, plans to use her, as promised, in *Strictly Dishonorable* were abandoned. Instead, another Broadway émigré, Sidney Fox, was given the part for *her* movie debut. Davis believes it was the result of her first encounter with studio head Carl Laemmle, Jr., who was clearly unimpressed with

HOLLYWOOD: THE EARLY YEARS (1930-1934)

the little wide-eyed girl from Broadway who wore no make-up except lipstick and kept her ash-blonde hair tied in a knot. She soon heard rumors that she was unofficially known on the Universal lot as "the little brown wren." Davis spent time being photographed in the portrait gallery, then was tested for a film. No script was involved; instead, she was required to lie on a couch while, one by one, some fifteen men made ardent love to her. One man, Gilbert Roland, reassured her: "Don't be upset. This is the picture business. We've all gone through it. Just relax!"

During the Christmas holidays she was tested for *Heart in Hand* (eventually released as *A House Divided*), a Walter Huston film, directed by William Wyler. However, the wardrobe department attired Davis in a low-cut cotton dress that prompted Wyler to comment, "What do you think of these girls who show their chests and think they can get jobs?" Davis says it made her too self-conscious to test well, and the role went to Helen

BAD SISTER (1931). With Emma Dunn, Sidney Fox, and Charles Winninger

SEED (1931). With Raymond Hackett and John Boles

Chandler.

Finally, she learned that she was being considered for *Gambling Daughters*, a film version of Booth Tarkington's *The Flirt*, opposite Conrad Nagel. But when the film went into production, Sidney Fox had the female lead, playing a hellraising siren, and Davis had a secondary role as her drab sister. But at least she was working, and in good company: Humphrey Bogart (his fourth film), ZaSu Pitts, Charles Winninger, Emma Dunn, Bert Roach, and her so-called lookalike, Slim Summerville. Davis says the film was unbelievably bad and so was she. *The New York Times* critic found her "too lugubrious" to hold audience sympathy in a "wooden and insecurely presented story of two sisters who should have known better in the first place." *Variety* was more favorable: "Bette Davis holds much promise in her handling of Laura—sweet, simple, and the very essence of repression." Before release—*Gambling Daughters* was retitled *Bad Sister* (1931). Davis later called it the worst experience of her life.

Surprisingly, when option time arrived, her contract was renewed for three months. The reason was not her performance in *Bad Sister*, but rather the rec-ommendation of that film's photographer, Karl Freund, who told Laemmle, "Davis has lovely eyes."

However, what Universal had in store for her was no better than *Bad Sister*. First, she was cast as one of the grown children of divorced parents John Boles and Lois Wilson in John M. Stahl's *Seed* (1931), a slowly paced family soap opera. Its source was a novel by Charles G. Norris advocating birth control, but aside from the film's title it gave little indication of dealing with so touchy a subject. Davis thinks her part could easily have been edited out.

The critics rather liked James Whale's film version of Robert E. Sherwood's poignant play *Waterloo Bridge* (1931), but barely noticed any of its cast, except for the two leading players, Mae Clarke (freshly recovered from James Cagney's famous grapefruit attack in *The Public Enemy*) and Kent Douglass (shortly before changing his name to Douglass Montgomery). Davis had a small, thankless ingenue role as the hero's enthusiastic younger sister. Today *Waterloo Bridge* is best known for its 1940 MGM remake with Vivien Leigh and Robert Taylor.

Again the powers at Universal scheduled Davis for a role and

WATERLOO BRIDGE (1931). With Enid Bennett, Kent Douglass, Mae Clarke, and Frederick Kerr

then changed their minds, and so Mae Clarke replaced her as the feminine lead in the now-classic *Frankenstein*. Instead, Universal farmed Davis out to RKO for a sentimental rural melodrama entitled *Other People's Business*, an unsuccessful attempt to capitalize on Phillips Lord's radio popularity as folksy Seth Parker. In this homespun tale of farmers, young romance, and small-town prejudice, Davis was teamed romantically with Frank Albertson, and she gave the ingenue role of Mary Lucy what little distinction it had. Released early in 1932, *Other People's Business* played most theatres as *Way Back Home*. Davis considers it the first movie in which she was well pho-

tographed (by J. Roy Hunt). The film showed care and expense, although the "New England" location scenes were shot at Santa Cruz.

She returned to her home studio and an empty schedule. Universal could not decide what to do with her—except loan her out again. This time Davis found herself overshadowed by an evil Natalie Moorhead in Columbia's *The Menace* (1932), a modest murder thriller, poorly adapted from Edgar Wallace's novel *The Feathered Serpent*. Davis claims the picture was filmed in eight days, and that her role consisted mainly of screams and faints as the various corpses materialized.

When her short-time contract expired, Universal decided not

to renew it. No other studio seemed interested. Her only job offer came from independent producer Benjamin F. Zeidman, who cast her opposite Pat O'Brien in a "poverty row" quickie called *Hell's House* (1932). (Originally released as *Juvenile Court*, the film provoked legal action from an irate Los Angeles exhibitor, who unknowingly booked *both* titles on one double-feature program.) Davis says *Hell's House* took about five minutes to make but seemed like an eternity, although she enjoyed acting opposite O'Brien and thought that the photography and editing were superior to Universal's. As the teen-aged hero's girl friend who turns to bootlegger O'Brien, she had little footage, since the film was more concerned with the hero's tangles with the law and reformatory life than with his romantic involvement.

After six motion pictures Bette Davis felt she was a failure and should return to New York to pick up the pieces of her acting career. The day before she and Ruthie were to return East there was a phone call from the renowned character actor George Arliss. Murray Kinnell, a supporting player in *The Menace*, had submitted her name to Arliss as a possibility for the ingenue lead in his next picture, *The Man Who Played God*. Could she, he asked, meet him the following afternoon at Warner Brothers to discuss the role?

Despite his age (sixty-four), his wizened appearance, and his eccentric acting style, George

WAY BACK HOME (1932). With Phillips Lord

Arliss was a popular Warners star. He had won an Academy Award for *Disraeli,* and such vehicles as *The Green Goddess, Old English,* and *Alexander Hamilton* were prestigious and financially successful films for the studio. So the prospect of playing opposite Arliss was exhilarating to Davis.

Davis and Arliss found immediate rapport. Their training in the legitimate theater, their dedication to the craft of acting, helped them to realize a unity of approach that assured Arliss he was right in selecting her for the film. Davis has called *The Man Who Played God* (1932) her most important picture. "I did others I liked better and which were far more significant," she reports, "but there was something about appearing as Mr. Arliss's leading lady which gave me standing."

Adapted from a short story by Gouverneur Morris and a play by Jules Eckert Goodman, *The Man Who Played God* concerns Royale (Arliss), a concert pianist who loses his hearing and learns to help others by reading lips. Davis was his fiancée Grace, who remains faithful to the musician despite her love for Harold (Donald Cook), a young man her own age. The plot is resolved when Royale eavesdrops on a meeting between Grace and Harold, realizes the girl plans to give up her future for him, and breaks their engagement, finding contentment with an older woman (Violet Heming) who has always loved him.

In *My Ten Years in the Studios,* George Arliss wrote, "I think that only two or three times in my experience have I ever got from an actor at rehearsal something beyond what I realized in the part. Bette Davis proved to be one of the exceptions. I knew she had a 'nice little part' important to me—so I hoped for the best. I did not expect anything but a nice little performance. But when we rehearsed, she startled me; the nice little part became a deep and vivid creation, and I felt rather humbled that this young girl had been able to discover and portray something that my imagination had failed to conceive. She startled me because, quite unexpectedly, I got from her a flash that illuminated mere words and inspired them with passion and emotion. That is the kind of light that cannot be hidden under a bushel."

For Bette Davis, George Arliss had played God. Not only had he assisted John Adolfi in her direction but he saw that care was taken with her make-up, coiffure, and wardrobe. Her "little

24

THE MENACE (1932). With Natalie Moorhead and H. B. Warner

HELL'S HOUSE (1932). With Pat O'Brien and Junior Durkin

THE MAN WHO PLAYED GOD (1932). With Violet Heming, George Arliss, and Louise Closser Hale

brown wren" period was in the past; she was now a stylish blonde whose intense performance impressed Warners enough to win her a long-term contract with the studio. *The New York Times* reviewer was not that impressed; his only comment on Davis was that she spoke "too loudly for the microphone."

Davis was then cast in the remake of Edna Ferber's durable novel, *So Big* (1932), which had served as a silent vehicle for Colleen Moore in 1925 and would be re-tailored for Jane Wyman in 1953. In the 1932 version Barbara Stanwyck, who had just moved to Warners from Columbia, had the role of noble Selina Peake, whose restless grown son (Hardie Albright) appears to

"find himself" when he falls in love with artist Dallas O'Mara (Davis). William A. Wellman directed smoothly and André Sennwald in *The New York Times* found the movie faithful to Miss Ferber's book but lacking in drama. Bette Davis was termed "unusually competent."

During the filming of *So Big* Davis learned about the workhorse schedules to which Warners often put their contractees. After working all day in the Stanwyck film she would commute to another set, where Ruth Chatterton was starring in *The Rich Are Always With Us* (1932), a drawing-room comedy of wealthy Manhattan sophisticates, in which Davis played a flashy young woman-about-town

26

SO BIG (1932). With Hardie Albright

THE RICH ARE ALWAYS WITH US (1932). With George Brent

THE DARK HORSE (1932). With Warren William and Frank McHugh

oddly named Malbro. She spent all her time during the film in hopeless pursuit of news correspondent George Brent, a young Irish actor who was also working in *So Big*, his first film for Warners. Davis and Brent later became good friends off the set and made nine more films together.

Faced with her first scene opposite Ruth Chatterton, Davis suffered such a case of nerves that she startled the seasoned actress with the spontaneous confession: "I'm so damned scared of you I'm speechless!" After that Chatterton went out of her way to help the young ingenue with her role, a kindness Davis herself has duplicated in recent years when acting with newcomers.

Her studio kept Davis sprinting from film to film during 1932. In quick succession she was one of a trio of school friends who met contrasting fates in *Three on a Match*, a loyal political worker in *The Dark Horse*, and a rich southern vamp in *Cabin in the Cotton*.

28

In *Three on a Match* she was a stenographer who compares notes with her chums on the events of the intervening years. Ann Dvorak had the meatiest role as the restless girl who marries a wealthy man (Warren William), descends to drugs and alcohol after their divorce, and finally kills herself in a desperate attempt to save her kidnapped son. Joan Blondell was the third girl, a singer who marries Warren William on the rebound.

Mervyn LeRoy directed *Three on a Match* with the same pace and vigor as his previous film, *The Public Enemy*, and the result is a typically enjoyable low-budget film from Warners. Davis reports that LeRoy barely acknowledged her presence, while pointedly praising Blondell. She believes that her stage background may have prompted his negative reaction.

Three on a Match gave short shrift to the Davis character, so that long before her scenes were completed she was working in *The Dark Horse* under Alfred E. Green's direction. Warren William, starring in *Three on a Match*, thought enough of her ability to request that she play opposite him in the new film. It was a lively political satire—one

THREE ON A MATCH (1932). With Joan Blondell and Ann Dvorak

of the few good comedies dealing with politics. In *The New York Times*, Mordaunt Hall lauded the Joseph Jackson-Wilson Mizner screenplay: "It is filled with bright lines and clever incidents and never a word nor an action is wasted." Hall thought that Davis gave "a splendid performance."

But it was *Cabin in the Cotton*, a Richard Barthelmess vehicle directed by the tough, demanding Michael Curtiz, that first cast Bette Davis in the type of conniving-vixen role that would account for much of her future popularity. As the seductive daughter of a wealthy planter, she flirted shamelessly with sharecropper Barthelmess and spoke such deathless Paul Green dialogue as the much-quoted "Ah'd luv to kiss yo, but ah jes washed mah hayuh" and "Yo haid's full o' playuns, isn't it, dahlin'—full o' playuns?"

Curtiz had been very definite about not wanting Davis for the role, but Warners production manager Darryl Zanuck had thought she'd be good in it, and over-ruled the director. Davis appreciated working in a good film with a literate script, but she says that Curtiz made her life hell every day she worked on it. Surprisingly, the actress and director agreed to work together

in five more films—and with great rapport.

Cast for the first time on the screen as a "bad" girl, Bette Davis displayed flashes of the brilliance with which she was to infuse some of her best work. Her seduction of Barthelmess—removing her dress casually as she sings "Minnie the Moocher" —is broadly played but vividly effective. Despite the fact that her role kept her off-screen for much of the action, there were those who felt she stole the movie's acting honors with her portrayal of a ripe Southern peach. Had Zanuck not insisted that she play Madge in *Cabin in the Cotton*, Davis might never have won the role that many consider her greatest—Mildred in *Of Human Bondage*.

On August 18, 1932, aged 24, Bette Davis became Mrs. Harmon O. Nelson, Jr., amidst the 115-degree heat of Yuma, Arizona, to which they had eloped. For their honeymoon trip they joined a multi-star, cross-country Warners junket on behalf of the lavish new musical, *42nd Street*, and tied in with the inauguration of Franklin D. Roosevelt. Despite the Depression the entourage traveled in luxury, and Davis surprised her studio's publicity staff with the extent of her popularity with the fans. As

CABIN IN THE COTTON (1932). With Richard Barthelmess

she states in her autobiography, it was indeed a "strange" honeymoon.

Davis was now matched with Spencer Tracy, one of the screen's finest actors, in a compelling crime drama, *20,000 Years in Sing Sing* (1933). Based on Warden Lewis E. Lawes' best-selling book about prison conditions, the film was dominated by Tracy's strong performance as a tough gangster imprisoned on a felony conviction, who escapes and becomes implicated in the murder of the mobster (Louis Calhern) responsible for sending him to Sing Sing. Davis played his girl, who shoots

Calhern with his own gun to save Tracy but is unable to convince anyone of her story. Tracy is convicted of murder and executed. As directed by Michael Curtiz, it made for a powerful and uncompromising melodrama, one of the first and best of Warners' prison films. Tracy and Davis worked so well together that they often talked of reteaming for another movie but never did.

By now Curtiz had apparently reversed his opinion of Bette Davis as an actress, for Wilson Mizner, co-author of the *20,000 Years in Sing Sing* screenplay, alerted her to the fact that Cur-

31

20,000 YEARS IN SING SING (1933). With Arthur Byron and Spencer Tracy

tiz had shown a print of *Cabin in the Cotton* to John Cromwell, who was to direct *Of Human Bondage*. And he added that producer David O. Selznick, who had bought the Somerset Maugham novel for RKO, reportedly considered Davis the logical choice for Mildred.

The actress finished 1932 with *Parachute Jumper*, one of the movies she now repeatedly scorns on television "talk" shows. It was her seventh Warner movie in less than ten months, an action yarn about a pilot who becomes innocently involved with narcotics smuggling. Cast opposite Douglas Fairbanks, Jr., Davis again used a thick Southern drawl to play Alabama, secretary-moll to mobster Leo Carrillo. A brief clip from *Parachute Jumper* turns up in Davis's 1962 thriller *What Ever Happened to Baby Jane?*

For her next film Davis was reunited with George Arliss in *The Working Man* (1933), the slight but ingratiating story of an aging businessman who takes a job in his own shoe factory in an effort to understand the younger generation. She played a reckless young rich girl who benefits from his influence and becomes a sober, responsible

PARACHUTE JUMPER (1933). With Frank McHugh, Leo Carrillo and Douglas Fairbanks, Jr.

THE WORKING MAN (1933). With George Arliss

EX-LADY (1933). With Kay Strozzi and Gene Raymond

secretary. The director was John Adolfi, who had guided Arliss and Davis through *The Man Who Played God.*

The Working Man marked a farewell to Bette Davis's supporting ingenue roles. Beginning with *Ex-Lady* in 1933, she was officially a star. Her vehicle, however, was ill-advised. Under Robert Florey's direction she played an emancipated commercial artist who is convinced that marriage spells doom for romance. When she changes her mind and agrees to marry her lover (Gene Raymond), there are many complications, none of them amusing. The subject mat-

ter was risque enough to interest the public, if not the critics, who deplored it. Davis calls it "a piece of junk" and says her shame was only exceeded by her fury.

Davis now learned that RKO would film *Mary of Scotland* with Katharine Hepburn and Fredric March. Hepburn was perhaps the one movie actress in her age range that Davis admired or envied. Always fascinated by books and plays about Elizabeth I, Davis went to see John Ford, without her studio's knowledge, hoping to persuade the director to cast her in the supporting role of Elizabeth.

Davis reports Ford merely laughed at her. March's wife, Florence Eldridge, played Queen Bess.

Bureau of Missing Persons (1933) brought Davis and Pat O'Brien together again, no longer working under the poverty-row circumstances of *Hell's House* but still far from gilt-edged surroundings. Davis was a falsely accused murderess, eluding the police under a pseudonym while trying to clear her name. O'Brien was the tough detective who helps her to prove her innocence and capture the true culprit. It was an odd film, veering between gallows humor and melodrama, but Roy Del Ruth's well-paced direction and some bristling, acerbic dialogue by Robert Presnell helped hold it together.

Davis now found that she was pregnant—a situation both her husband and mother considered unfortunate. Nelson, who was vainly struggling to remain the family breadwinner, refused to have her pay the hospital bills for her own child. He and Ruthie also felt that a baby at this time would seriously hamper her career. Although admittedly heartsick, Davis consented to an abortion, and then plunged into a hectic year of film-making in 1934.

Fashions of 1934 cast Davis

BUREAU OF MISSING PERSONS (1933). With Pat O'Brien

FASHIONS OF 1934 (1934). With William Powell and Phillip Reed

opposite suave William Powell in a sophisticated comedy-drama about duplicity among rival fashion designers in Paris. Davis now laughs at the glamour job performed on her by both the make-up and wardrobe departments for this film, in which she played a model who was also an artist and assistant to fashion-swindler Powell. William Dieterle, whose forte was serious drama, directed. The film's highlights were a fashion display and a lavish Busby Berkeley production number of "Spin a Little Web of Dreams"—which had nothing to do with her or Powell.

The Big Shakedown (1934) is typical of the Davis films of this period—briskly paced, trimmed to little more than an hour, and pointlessly entertaining. In this racketeer melodrama she was married to Charles Farrell, a pharmacist caught up in gangster Ricardo Cortez's drug racket. With platinum hair, Davis could do little but look attractive as she endured one traumatic experience after another, including nearly dying in childbirth.

In *Jimmy the Gent* (1934), filmed under the title *Always a Gent*, she played second fiddle to James Cagney in a fast-talk-

THE BIG SHAKEDOWN (1934). With Allen Jenkins

JIMMY THE GENT (1934). With James Cagney

FOG OVER FRISCO (1934). With Margaret Lindsay and
Arthur Byron

ing farce about another kind of racket—ruthless exploiters who hunt for missing heirs. Davis played his employee and girl friend who, upset by his business tactics, goes to work for his competitor (Alan Dinehart). Her role wasn't the size of Cagney's, but the press liked her performance. Again, Michael Curtiz directed efficiently.

William Dieterle's *Fog Over Frisco* (1934), another yarn about gangsters and their victims, cast Bette Davis as a

thrill-seeking society girl who mixes with the mob and winds up a corpse long before the denouement. The actress gave her part more intensity than the script warranted, indicating that she was fully capable of more than routine roles in assembly-line films.

Housewife (1934), directed by Alfred E. Green, remains among Davis's least favorite Warner memories of the mid-thirties. She played the office siren who comes between a reasonably happy young couple (George Brent and Ann Dvorak). The straying husband returns home after he injures his son accidentally and realizes that he still loves his steadfast wife.

Davis reports she was allowed "some dramatic range" in *Bordertown* (1935), a well-made melodrama which gave Paul Muni, as a Mexican lawyer, the most footage and an opportunity for some blatant overacting in the eye-flashing, Rudolph Valentino manner. Though given to some risible pelvic flouncing,

Davis gave the film's best performance as the faithless wife of casino owner Eugene Pallette. In hopes of winning Muni's affections, Davis precipitates her husband's death, is spurned by Muni, implicates him in Pallette's murder, and gets them both imprisoned. On the witness stand, the strain of confinement and the prosecution's cross-examination take their toll; she goes berserk and is led away in a state of shock.

For Bette Davis, it was the first film in which Warners had

HOUSEWIFE (1934). With George Brent

BORDERTOWN (1935). With Paul Muni

given her a really strong leading role in a well-written (Laird Doyle-Wallace Smith) script. But she had to battle with director Archie Mayo to maintain the integrity of her interpretation. In her final scenes he wanted her to "play insanity" in silent-movie style, while Davis opted for a more subtle approach. Argued Mayo, "They'll never know you're supposed to be insane." Davis prevailed upon Warners production head Darryl Zanuck to allow the preview audience to be the judge. She got her wish,

that audience was convinced and she heard no more about it. In *The New York Times*, André Sennwald praised her "fine and uncommonly honest" performance, adding that she was "effective and touching in pathological mazes which the cinema rarely dares to examine."

Although made before *Of Human Bondage* in 1934, *Bordertown* was not released until January of the following year, after the Maugham story had reached the screen.

Of *Human Bondage* (1934) would seem to offer, in the character of Mildred, a part that any actress would forfeit her soul to play. However, Bette Davis recalls that the character was so disagreeable that none of Hollywood's established stars were interested. With the knowledge that director John Cromwell wanted to borrow her from Warners for the role, Davis became obsessed with getting it. Her studio refused to loan her to RKO, so she waged a nuisance campaign. Every day for six months she badgered Jack Warner. Finally, if only to rid himself of her persistent hounding, he relented.

"My employers," says Davis, "believed I would hang myself playing such an unpleasant heroine. I think they identified me with the character and felt we deserved one another!"

Davis says she never worked harder on any role than she did on Mildred. She knew it could make or break her movie career. Cromwell's faith, in wanting her for the role, helped considerably. To study the cockney accent she hired an English wardrobe woman to move in with her.

Maugham's Mildred is an attractive but sluttish waitress who enthralls club-footed medical student Philip Carey (Leslie

ACTING TRIUMPH (1934-1936)

Howard), rejects him because he's crippled, but later seeks his aid when she finds herself pregnant but unwed. After the baby arrives Mildred trades on Carey's obsession with her, moving in and out of his life as it suits her convenience, between men. Eventually, she contracts syphilis and dies in a charity ward.

The critics were enthusiastic about Davis's portrayal. *Life* magazine called it "probably the best performance ever recorded on the screen by a U.S. actress," while in *The New York Times* Mordaunt Hall wrote, "Bette Davis provides what is easily her finest performance." Seen today, in the light of more subtle contemporary acting and directing styles, Davis's Mildred occasionally seems too mannered and overwrought. Her bravura performance undoubtedly grips the attention, but in her tirades against Philip Carey, Davis seems out of control and makes it very difficult to understand why so cultured a gentleman would tolerate such a guttersnipe for so long. Still, *Of*

OF HUMAN BONDAGE (1934). As Mildred Rogers

Human Bondage proved a major triumph—for RKO, which had gambled with Bette Davis and won, and for the actress herself, who now believed that Warners would reward her with good roles in first-rate scripts.

When Davis failed to receive an Academy Award nomination for Best Actress, Warners launched a "write-in" campaign in the trade papers. Davis gained valuable publicity but that was all. The award that year went to Claudette Colbert for her performance in *It Happened One Night*.

After her triumph in *Of Human Bondage*, Warners welcomed her back with a Perry Mason mystery, *The Case of the Howling Dog*, which she adamantly refused. (Mary Astor took the role.) She was then handed such forgettable scripts as *The Girl From 10th Avenue*,

OF HUMAN BONDAGE (1934). With Leslie Howard

Front Page Woman and *Special Agent*. She filmed them all, but not without raising dust. Davis says: "There was no change in the Warner attitude after all this acclaim. I was made to trudge through the professional swamp at Warners, brimming over with frustration and rage. One skirmish after another followed *Bondage*."

With tightly coiffured blonde curls and some of the least attractive tailored frocks of the mid-Thirties, she went through the trio of films like a prison sentence. In *The Girl From 10th Avenue* (1935), directed by Alfred E. Green, she was a tenement shopgirl who tries to rehabilitate, and eventually marries, an alcoholic society lawyer (Ian Hunter). Ironically, when this film opened at New York's Capi-

tol Theater, the stage show featured a ·one-act play *The Open Door*, starring the distinguished actress who once rejected Bette Davis as a student—Eva Le Gallienne.

If *Front Page Woman* and *Special Agent* (both 1935) seem like one and the same film, it might be because both cast Davis, in a parade of drab outfits, opposite George Brent, and both involved her with crime. In the former, she was a "sob sister" for a daily paper, engaged to the top reporter of a rival paper (Brent), who thinks "women make bum newspapermen." She disproves his theory by solving a murder case. Many of the lines had a sharp bite that made for amusing repartee between the actors. *Special Agent* was produced by William Ran-

43

THE GIRL FROM 10TH AVENUE (1935). With Ian Hunter

dolph Hearst's Cosmopolitan Pictures for Warners release. (This might explain why Davis now resembled Marion Davies.) Here she played the bookkeeper of a syndicate operated by gangster Ricardo Cortez. Brent was a Treasury agent masquerading as a reporter. Under William Keighley's direction the story moved swiftly, but the film was totally without distinction and Davis's nerves were fraying rapidly.

Davis reports she was "punch-drunk" by the time the studio gave her Laird Doyle's screenplay of *Dangerous*. She played Joyce Heath, a bottle-swigging, once-famous stage actress hellbent on her own destruction—until an admiring architect (Franchot Tone) befriends her and sponsors a theatrical comeback. Unfortunately, the star

has a secret husband (John Eldredge), and when he refuses her a divorce so she can marry the architect, Joyce attempts to kill them both by driving into a tree. As in Edith Wharton's *Ethan Frome*, they both survive, though he is crippled for life. Joyce returns to the stage in triumph, sacrificing love (Tone) for duty (Eldredge).

Alfred E. Green directed this uneven soap opera, and Davis gave a performance of extraordinary intensity. Indeed, viewed today, Davis's Joyce Heath is so highly charged, so kinetic and mannered as to be, at times, almost laughable. Yet in other scenes she is quite moving, as in her first encounter with Tone in which she tells him about her ill-starred past and her belief that she jinxes everyone who knows her. She also has some scenes of

FRONT PAGE WOMAN (1935). With J. Carroll Naish

SPECIAL AGENT (1935). With George Brent

harsh comedy with Alison Skipworth, playing a housekeeper who is righteously disgusted by Joyce's drinking.

Davis says she considered the *Dangerous* screenplay "maudlin and mawkish, with a pretense at quality," and that she "worked like ten men" to make something of it. That year Bette Davis was among six Best Actress nominees for the Academy Award. Her competition was Elisabeth Bergner in *Escape Me Never*; Claudette Colbert in *Private Worlds*; Katharine Hepburn in *Alice Adams*; Miriam Hopkins in *Becky Sharp* and Merle Oberon in *The Dark Angel*.

Davis still believes that the Oscar she won for *Dangerous* was a consolation prize for losing out with *Of Human Bondage*. In her opinion Hepburn gave the best performance of 1935 and *she* deserved the statuette. This was the first of what came to be known as the "Holdover" awards —a belated prize for work unrewarded the previous year.

Although Davis says she was the one who gave the Academy's gold statuette the nickname "Oscar" (because it looked like the backside of her husband, whose middle name was Oscar), two others also claimed that inspiration. The matter has never been settled.

The Petrified Forest, her first film for 1936, again gave Davis a decent part in a major Warners movie. Leslie Howard repeated his stage performance in the Robert E. Sherwood melodrama and insisted that the studio hire Humphrey Bogart to re-create *his* stage role of the psychopathic gangster, Duke Mantee. Warners, which already had Edward G. Robinson and James Cagney under contract, agreed reluctantly. Davis got the role Peggy Conklin had created on Broadway—Gaby Maple, a romantic-minded girl who longs to escape her arid life in the Arizona desert cafe run by her father. Onto the scene comes Alan Squier (Howard), a burned-out intellectual with a death wish. Gaby falls in love with him, but her idyll is short-lived when the murderous Duke Mantee and his henchmen, fleeing from the police, arrive on the scene and keep everyone prisoners in the cafe. At the climax Alan forces Mantee to shoot him, and Gaby is left with Alan's insurance policy—money that will enable her to study art in Paris.

Though largely a photographed stage play in which the Sherwood symbolism (intellectual and killer both die in

DANGEROUS (1935). With Franchot Tone

THE PETRIFIED FOREST (1936). With Leslie Howard

barren desert) is somewhat too obvious, the film benefits from fine performances and the restrained direction of Archie Mayo. As Squier, Leslie Howard is sensitive and moving, delicately conveying the sadness and resignation of the character. As Mantee, Bogart proved a sensation, revitalizing his unmemorable screen career. And Davis took full advantage of the opportunity to play a simple romantic girl, plainly dressed and free of neurotic tics and quirks. She is genuinely touching as she yearns for Paris or reacts with awe to Alan Squier's tenderness and concern.

The Davis career now took another downward dive with a frothy Cinderella comedy entitled *The Golden Arrow* (1936), opposite George Brent. With her hair darkened to its natural ash-blonde for the first time in years, Davis portrayed Daisy Appleby, a former restaurant cashier hired by a cosmetics firm to impersonate a madcap heiress. By this time madcap heiresses, even fake ones, were beginning to seem old-fashioned, and with a script suggested by Michael Arlen's *The Green Hat*, itself a musty affair, *The Golden Arrow* sank into oblivion.

The brothers Warner then assigned her to *Satan Met a Lady*

(1936), the second, and by far the worst, of the three versions yet filmed of Dashiell Hammett's mystery novel *The Maltese Falcon*. (The 1931 version starred Ricardo Cortez and Bebe Daniels.) In the role roughly equivalent to Mary Astor's Brigid O'Shaughnessy five years later, Davis was required to play a murderous femme fatale in a ludicrous crosscurrent of double-dealing and murder. So inferior was this film that it is difficult to fathom why Warners would have considered a remake in 1941.

Bette Davis took one look at Brown Holmes's screenplay and exploded. To Jack Warner she raged that she had served her apprenticeship and proven her ability many times over, and now she was justifiably outraged at still being burdened with scripts like *Satan Met a Lady*. Somehow Warners managed to pacify her with promises of a rosy Warners future if only she would proceed with the film, which she did, begrudgingly.

The story made so little sense that *The New York Times* critic dismissed it completely as "a cynical farce of elaborate and sustained cheapness." And he remarked that "a Bette Davis Reclamation Project to prevent the waste of this gifted lady's

49

THE GOLDEN ARROW (1936). With George Brent and Catherine Doucet

talents would not be a too-drastic addition to our various programs for the conservation of natural resources." For the moment, Davis's career was at its lowest ebb since *Hell's House* and *The Menace*.

Her reward for submitting to the indignities of *Satan Met a Lady* was a script entitled *God's Country and the Woman*, again opposite George Brent. Davis balked. She asked, instead, to play in the studio's *Anthony Adverse* but was turned down; they insisted she make *God's Country and the Woman*. Davis says the character—a lady lumberjack—was "an insufferable bore." After thirty-one films and an Oscar, she refused to let her hard-won career wash down the Warners drain with B pictures. She says: "If I never acted again in my life, I was not going to play in *God's Country*. It was now a matter of my own self respect."

Jack Warner now attempted to talk her into making the film with the comment that he had just optioned a new novel about the South, *Gone With the Wind*, and that she would have the lead in it. "Yes," retorted his rebellious star, "and I'll just bet

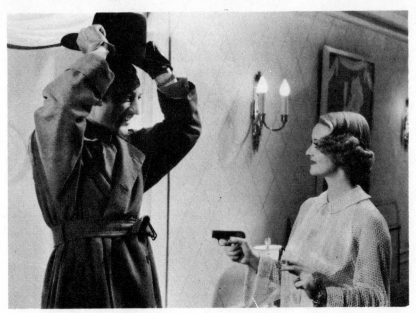

SATAN MET A LADY (1936). With Warren William

it's a dilly!"

She immediately staged a one-woman strike and retired to Laguna Beach. Warners replaced her in *God's Country and the Woman* with a new contractee named Beverly Roberts, and put their uncompromising star on a three-month suspension. She was given two more scripts, *Garden of the Moon* and *Comet Over Broadway*, which only angered her further. And she issued a statement to the press: "If I continue to appear in mediocre pictures, I'll have no career worth fighting for."

As time passed, the Warner-Davis breach widened and deepened. And when Italian-born British film mogul Ludovico Toeplitz made her an offer, she accepted. The deal: for twenty thousand pounds apiece she would star in two films—with script approval! The first would be *I'll Take the Low Road*, to be made in Italy with Douglass Montgomery and Nigel Bruce, followed by another in France, opposite Maurice Chevalier. With her family's full approval Davis signed with Toeplitz, and she and her husband sailed for England.

51

Ludovico Toeplitz had been associated with Alexander Korda in the production of two prestigious films, *The Private Life of Henry VIII* and *Catherine the Great*, and subsequently had branched out on his own to produce *The Love Affair of the Dictator*, with Clive Brook, and *Beloved Vagabond* with Maurice Chevalier. To Bette Davis, his offer seemed the perfect answer to her problems with Warners.

She and Ham arrived in Britain on their fourth anniversary. At once Warners served her with an injunction prohibiting her from working anywhere. Jack Warner met with Toeplitz, and they argued about her two contracts. Toeplitz considered his agreement with Davis completely legal. Warner took his case into the English courts and engaged Sir Patrick Hastings, one of Britain's great legal minds. Toeplitz recommended that Davis engage a brilliant lawyer named Sir William Jowett—at a retainer fee of ten thousand dollars. Her suspension was already costing her a fortune, and the prospect of an expensive court battle was depressing.

Ham Nelson returned to the United States to look for employment, leaving his wife's morale at low ebb. During the trial Bette Davis was made to

DAVIS VERSUS WARNERS (1936-1938)

seem like a naughty child who had ungratefully turned on the family that had raised her. In her own defense she pointed out that all she wanted was better roles that would reflect the full development of her acting talents. The trial was well publicized and closely followed by the entire movie industry.

Warners won the case. Justice Branson weighed both sides of the argument and ruled that although the studio had not violated its agreement, Bette Davis had. And Branson's reaction to the high salaries earned by American film stars was completely unsympathetic; he called them exorbitant, declaring that anybody could endure "artistic hardship" under those circumstances.

Davis had lost a courageous battle and a very expensive one, for the law obliged her to pay Warners' court fees as well as her own. And she had now forfeited a fortune in salary because of her absence. She was determined to appeal the decision. The case had already cost her in excess of thirty thousand dollars;

MARKED WOMAN (1937). With Eduardo Ciannelli

an appeal would raise the sum to fifty thousand. Davis stayed on in her Sussex hotel, taking long walks and pondering her fate back at Warner Brothers. Unexpectedly, she received a visit from George Arliss. Davis reports that his advice was what she needed: "Go back gracefully and accept the decision. You haven't lost as much as you think."

In November 1936, Davis returned to the States. Her husband and mother met her in New York. Ham had cut a record with Tommy Dorsey, and the couple agreed he should remain in Manhattan and keep trying there. Bette and Ruthie left for Hollywood where they were met with an unexpectedly cordial reception at Warners. Not only did the studio pay for their part of the trial, but they agreed to split Sir William's re-

tainer with her. Davis knew that the studio would never have taken such a chance had they not realized the actress's seriousness about her career. Obviously they were impressed with her performance in England. "In a way," Davis says, "my defeat was a victory. At last we were seeing eye to eye on my career." The film industry appeared to respect her action.

Consequently, Davis was surprised to get a good role in a worthwhile picture, *Marked Woman* (1937). It was a tough underworld melodrama reflecting the concern that Warners dramas often showed for social injustice during the thirties. In this instance, a blistering Robert Rossen-Abem Finkel screenplay used the recent trial of vice racketeer Charles (Lucky) Luciano to focus on the career problems of clip-joint girls.

Davis played Mary Dwight, a self-sufficient cabaret hostess employed by mobster Johnny Vanning (Eduardo Ciannelli). At a Vanning party Mary's innocent younger sister (Jane Bryan) is killed for resisting rape, which shocks Mary and her fellow hostesses into open rebellion against their boss. Mary threatens to tell the authorities about Vanning's racket, and he retaliates by having her beaten and disfigured. Through the efforts of a sympathetic attorney (Humphrey Bogart) the girls testify in court and Vanning is convicted.

Lloyd Bacon, a Warners regular who had alternated between Cagney action pictures and musicals like *42nd Street*, directed efficiently, and although the red-light background of the story was restricted by Hays Office censorship, *Marked Woman* came as close to reality as restrictions would permit. The movie belongs mainly to the women in its cast, with Mayo Methot particularly good as a desperate aging "hostess." Bette Davis is vivid in the sort of high-strung, neurotic role she had not had since *Dangerous*, and Ciannelli's chilling portrait of a ruthless gangster is one not easily forgotten.

Variety was impressed with Davis's characterization and had this to say about her talent: "She is among the Hollywood few who can submerge themselves in a role to the point where they become the character they are playing. Her performance here is also rife with subtleties of expression and gesture."

Despite the frankness of contemporary films much of *Marked Woman* still holds up, although some of Davis's acting does not; in one or two scenes she speaks so rapidly that the ear can barely keep up with her, and she achieves transitions of mood and character with the unbelievable speed of mercury. But in 1937 the critics were more easily pleased; in *The New York Times* Frank S. Nugent wrote, "Miss Davis has turned in her best performance since she cut Leslie Howard to the quick in *Of Human Bondage*."

Kid Galahad (1937) put her in support of Wayne Morris (a newcomer, playing the title role), Edward G. Robinson and Humphrey Bogart in a rugged prizefight melodrama, directed by Michael Curtiz. Columnists had predicted Davis would turn down the part of Fluff, fight-manager Robinson's mistress, who falls for the Kid but loses him to a younger girl (Jane Bryan) and walks off into the fog

54

KID GALAHAD (1937). With Edward G. Robinson and Harry Carey

THAT CERTAIN WOMAN (1937). With Ian Hunter

alone, after Robinson and Bogart kill each other in a gun battle. Davis surprised them by stating, "*Kid Galahad*, while not giving me much of a role in the artistic sense, has such a lot of good robust fight stuff in it that it is bound to appeal to a totally different cinema audience, an audience with which I nevertheless need to be kept in touch."

As usual, Davis was right. Although her part was subordinate to the others, and the film concentrated on some unusually brutal boxing scenes, she gave her role such warmth and humor that she appeared to hold the story together. Her conciliatory scenes with the temperamental Robinson, her muted expressions of love for Morris, gave the character more depth than it deserved.

Davis completed 1937 with two pictures that are not among her best-remembered: the sudsy *That Certain Woman* and *It's Love I'm After*, which offered the actress a rare comedy part opposite Leslie Howard.

The former was a remake of *The Trespasser*, a Gloria Swanson vehicle first filmed eight years earlier. *Time* magazine, noting that Davis was more cooperative with Warners since her court battle, observed: "In less precarious times, the role she is

given in *That Certain Woman* might conceivably have evoked renewed protest from her, not that it lacks scope for her remarkable dramatic range, but because it heaps tragedy upon her with Sophoclean relentlessness, and because its wearying, buskined tread cannot pretend to vie with her more smartly-stepping 1937 successes, *Marked Woman* and *Kid Galahad*."

The film marked Davis's first collaboration with Edmund Goulding, who later directed two of her finest performances in *Dark Victory* and *The Old Maid*. Henry Fonda and Ian Hunter were her co-stars in a screenplay (also by Goulding) in which she played a bootlegger's young widow who tries to hide her notoriety and becomes a secretary to a lawyer, an unhappily married man who falls in love with her. The plot then takes her through an obstacle course of marriage, scandal, annulment, unwed motherhood and eventual happiness with Fonda.

Through all these tribulations Davis managed to retain her professional aplomb, giving some conviction to emotional scenes in which she was required to defend her right to retain her child, born out of an annulled marriage, or to declare her love

IT'S LOVE I'M AFTER (1937). With Leslie Howard

for the wealthy Fonda, who is saddled with an invalid wife. The film was competently made, but Davis must have been wondering if she would ever be given a truly superior script in which she could test her mettle.

It's Love I'm After cast her and Leslie Howard as a successful theatrical team, Joyce Arden and Basil Underwood, whose offstage romance is hampered by fits of egotism, jealousy and petty quarrels. The frothy plot has Basil trying to discourage the attentions of an effusive debutante (Olivia de Havilland) and return her to the arms of her fiance (Patric Knowles). Eventually, Joyce gets Basil to the altar. Davis says that she and Howard enjoyed making this picture.

Under Archie Mayo's direction the comedy was reasonably amusing, with a Casey Robinson script that kept things spinning. Davis and Howard were clearly happy to be released, even for a brief time, from the bondage of tear-drenched dramas, and they responded with skillful, though slightly shrill, performances, particularly in their battle scenes. They were given some much-needed help by Eric Blore as Howard's manservant and George Barbier as de Havilland's befuddled father. Today *It's Love I'm After* seems only slightly amusing and, at times, downright tedious.

Davis now felt that she would do well to limit her screen appearances to two pictures a year. That way audiences might be less likely to tire of seeing her, and she could concentrate (she hoped, with Warners cooperation) on stories of consequence.

Obtaining the script of Paul Muni's next Warners film, *The Life of Emile Zola*, she became intrigued with the small part of the street girl, Nana, which she begged Jack Warner to let her play. She thinks that at that stage of her career it would have proved a sensational stunt. But neither Warner nor Muni would consider it. The role went to Erin O'Brien-Moore.

Recalling Jack Warner's 1936 promise that Davis would have the lead in *Gone With the Wind* if she made *God's Country and the Woman*, the actress says

that she had a second opportunity to play Scarlett O'Hara when David O. Selznick, who had purchased the property from Warners while Davis was in London, asked her studio if he could borrow her and Errol Flynn for the leads, as a package deal. The thought of Flynn as Rhett Butler, she says, "appalled her." She refused.

Instead she got *Jezebel* (1938) and another Academy Award. As a play by Owen Davis this romantic drama of the Old South had run for a scant thirty-two performances during the 1933-34 Broadway season. Miriam Hopkins had starred as Julie, a determined belle not unlike the heroine of *Gone With the Wind*. For Davis, getting Julie was the next-best consolation for losing Scarlett. At last she had the benefit of a soundly constructed script by Clement Ripley, Abem Finkel and—later known as a leading director—John Huston. She would be photographed by her favorite cinematographer, Ernest Haller. In her first costume picture she would have the opportunity to wear beautiful ante-bellum gowns designed by Orry-Kelly. And the director was William Wyler. Though she was first "stunned" to be placed in the hands of the brusque little man who had prevented her

JEZEBEL (1938). With Henry Fonda

being in *A House Divided*, she learned to work well with him and can still offer only the highest praise for his ability: "It was *he* who helped me realize my full potential as an actress. This man was a perfectionist and had the courage of twenty. He was as dedicated as I. It is impossible to describe the contribution that Wyler made to *Jezebel*."

Davis plays willful Julie Marsden whose actions are motivated by her unsuccessful efforts to win Pres Dillard (Henry Fonda), the one man she loves. In the film's most memorable sequence Julie appears at the 1850 Olympus Ball in New Orleans dressed in a red gown—a deliberate disregard for the white dresses traditionally worn by all unmarried young ladies. When she humiliates not only herself but Pres as well, he refuses to escort her home, forcing her instead to continue dancing with him across a ballroom floor deliberately cleared by the shocked citizenry. He breaks their engagement, and three years pass in which Julie secludes herself, waiting for him to return and marry her. When word arrives that he is coming back, she dresses in the white gown that she should have worn to the ball, as a symbol of her contrition. But Pres brings a wife (Margaret Lindsay) with him, and Julie is morally defeated. When Pres falls victim to a yellow-fever epidemic and is evacuated to a quarantined island, Julie accompanies him, promising his wife that if Pres lives she will send him back to her.

Jezebel is a lavish, well-produced film that withstands the passage of time due to the excellence of its direction, acting, and production values. Unlike the previous Davis movies it is not dated by its costuming or

59

make-up, and its performances are kept well in line by the demanding William Wyler. Davis's performance is flamboyant in her best style and the first to give evidence of a growing maturity and professionalism. She carried off a number of effective scenes, startling the guests at her party by leaping into the room dressed in a riding habit, pleading with her ex-beau to forgive her for her inexcusable behavior three years earlier, or begging Pres's wife to let her take him to the quarantined island.

The film and Davis were well received. (The actress must have been especially pleased by *Life* magazine's comment that she gave "a performance for the future Scarlett O'Hara to shoot at.") When she was presented with her second Academy Award, she gave full credit to director William Wyler. *Jezebel* also won nominations for Best Picture, Haller's photography, and Max Steiner's typically lush score. Fay Bainter, who played Julie's sympathetic Aunt Belle, won the Oscar for Best Supporting Actress.

One incident involving the making of *Jezebel* reflects Davis's tenacity against difficult odds. During production *Jezebel* had fallen so far behind its shooting schedule that Jack Warner decided to replace Wyler with another director. She went to Warner, told him that it would be a tragedy if the change were made, offered to work late if he were retained, and threatened to leave the picture if Wyler were fired. She got her way, and she reports that she

JEZEBEL (1938). With Margaret Lindsay

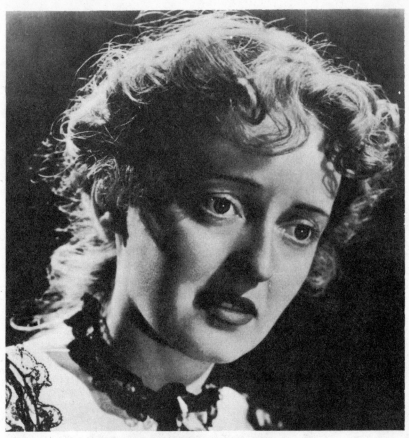

THE SISTERS (1938). As Louise Elliott Medlin.

often worked until midnight on that set, always returning early the following day. She says, "I earned the Oscar I won for *Jezebel.*"

With two Academy Awards and a court battle behind her, Bette Davis now faced her future at Warners with complete confidence. *Jezebel* made a lot of money for the studio, and Davis felt completely justified in asking for a raise. She got it, plus another chance at the script of *Comet Over Broadway*—which she once again rejected. The studio then assigned her to a sturdy costume drama, *The Sisters* (1938), opposite Errol Flynn, who played Frank Medlin, an unsuccessful newspaperman in old San Francisco. Davis was Louise Elliott, one of three sisters from a Montana mining town, who marries Frank on short notice and then has to face his alcoholism and jealousy. He disappears on a tramp steamer, returning after three years in the Orient to ask Louise for a second chance. She welcomes him back.

The movie's best sequence was devoted to the celebrated 1906 earthquake staged so memorably two years earlier in MGM's *San Francisco*. Though briefer and less ambitious than the 1936 movie, *The Sisters'* disaster scenes are handsomely executed. Davis reports that director Ana-tole Litvak put her through some perilous paces, with no thought given to a double. Despite the hazards she came through with what *The New York Times* called "a particularly lovely performance," adding some needed strength to Milton Krims' screenplay.

In December of 1938 Davis and Ham Nelson were divorced. The constant separations made necessary by their respective careers, plus the overwhelming factor of her great success, had caused their marriage to fail. The reasons were not unfamiliar in Hollywood's marital playground.

THE SISTERS (1938). With Errol Flynn

Davis's next film, *Dark Victory* (1939), gave her one of her best roles and the one probably best remembered by the public. Adapted by Casey Robinson from a Tallulah Bankhead vehicle that had played for only fifty-one performances during the Broadway winter of 1934, it was a first-rate tear-jerker about a headstrong heiress, Judy Traherne, who discovers that she has a brain tumor. Following a successful operation she and her doctor, Frederick Steele (George Brent), fall in love. When Judy learns that her operation was only partially successful, that she will be dead within a year, she rejects the doctor's affection as pity, and embarks on a round of fast living. Finally, the down-to-earth advice of her stableman (Humphrey Bogart) convinces Judy that she should accept affection and happiness while she can, and she marries her doctor. In the moving final sequence, realizing that her death is imminent, Judy sends her husband away to attend a medical convention, while she and her best friend, Ann (Geraldine Fitzgerald), plant a flower bed. As her vision fails, she sends Ann away ("Be my best friend! Go now! Please!") and enters the house, bidding good-bye to her two dogs and ascending to her

THE VINTAGE YEARS (1939-1944)

bedroom to face the end nobly. Davis's handling of this difficult scene is superb, and one might only carp at the angelic choirs with which composer Max Steiner saw fit to crown his Oscar-nominated score.

Judy Traherne is a marvelous part for any actress worth her salt, and Bette Davis caught every one of the character's wildly shifting moods as she went from the reckless, defiant young socialite ("I'm well and strong and nothing can touch me!") to the embittered hedonist, to the loving wife, resigned to brief happiness with the man she loves. Responding to Edmund Goulding's sensitive direction, she managed to keep the strong soap-opera aspects of the story under reasonably firm control. The film contains George Brent's favorite role, and is the one in which he thinks Davis gave "the greatest performance of her life." In *The New York Times* Frank S. Nugent called her "enchanting" and "superb," and stated that she deserved her 1938 Oscar less for *Jezebel* than for *Dark Victory*. She received a nomination but lost, ironically, to Vivien Leigh for her performance as Scarlett O'Hara.

Considering the film's success, it is interesting to learn how hard Davis fought to get Warners to take a chance on *Dark Victory*. Although he reluctantly bought the property for her, Jack Warner maintained his doubts even after shooting began: "Who's going to want to see a picture about a girl who dies?" Upset by her divorce during the filming, Davis says she offered to give up the role when she believed that she wasn't doing justice to it. Producer Hal Wallis's advice to her: "Stay upset."

Her next film, *Juarez* (1939), was a lavish historical epic about the Mexican leader Benito Pablo Juarez (Paul Muni), who led his people in a revolt against France in the 1860s. Davis's role as the Empress Carlotta was actually subordinate to Muni's, and she has claimed that her co-star (with whom she shared no scenes) was responsible for excising some of her footage to make room for fifty additional pages of script that would enlarge his own role. Davis's scenes opposite Brian Aherne as her ineffectual husband, the Archduke Maximilian, were completed even before Muni stepped before the cameras. As a result, *Juarez*

DARK VICTORY (1939). With George Brent

DARK VICTORY (1939). With Geraldine Fitzgerald

could have made *two* complete motion pictures. However, Muni's power at the studio won out. Davis believes that his actions prevented a good film from being a great one.

In a black wig and some handsome period costumes Bette Davis, as a woman who sees her well-meaning husband betrayed and finally executed, won praise for the suppression of her by-now obvious mannerisms and her convincing delineation of insanity. One of the film's best scenes had her frantically appealing for help, madly convinced that Napoleon (Claude Rains) was Satan incarnate, determined to kill her.

JUAREZ (1939). As the Empress Carlotta

Apparently, the brothers Warner liked their leading actress in costume roles, for they assigned her next to play the long-suffering Charlotte Lovell of Zoë Akins's play *The Old Maid* (1939), closely followed by an opportunity to impersonate her idolized Good Queen Bess in *The Private Lives of Elizabeth and Essex* (1939). Faced with the competition of Lillian Hellman's powerful drama *The Children's Hour*, it is difficult to comprehend how Miss Akins' maudlin adaptation of Edith Wharton's *The Old Maid* ever won her the coveted 1934-35 Pulitzer Prize. However, Casey Robinson's screenplay was a defi-

JUAREZ (1939). With Gale Sondergaard and Claude Rains

nite improvement. Guided by Edmund Goulding's firm, assured direction, and with Davis suffering superbly through an unfulfilled love affair, unwed motherhood and aging spinsterhood, the result was a four-handkerchief picture of great appeal to women. Warners had bought the property from Paramount, considering it an admirable vehicle for their reigning dramatic star. As expected, Bette Davis disappointed no one. Her Charlotte was a richly detailed portrait of an essentially loving woman who is forced by circumstances to harden into a sour, disapproving spinster. Actresses studying their craft would do well to watch Davis in

her principal scenes in this film: swaying to an inaudible waltz after she hears her daughter (who believes her to be her maiden aunt) exclaim angrily that "she's never danced!"; confronting her cousin Delia (Miriam Hopkins) in a staircase "showdown" on her daughter's wedding day ("Tonight she belongs to me! Tonight I want her to call me mother!"); finally saying good-bye to the girl who will never know the truth about the "old maid."

As originally written, cousin Delia was a selfish and conniving woman. However, as played by Hopkins, the character now seemed gentler and more charming. Davis says Hopkins loathed

THE OLD MAID (1939). With Miriam Hopkins

playing so unsympathetic a role and made the picture living hell for Davis by repeatedly attempting to upstage her, spoiling take after take of Davis's big scenes with silly interruptions and by behaving in a highly unprofessional way. "Miriam is a perfectly charming woman, socially," Davis says, adding, "Working with her is another story."

Without a rest Davis now went into the heavy costumes and bizarre make-up of playwright Maxwell Anderson's *Elizabeth the Queen*. To accommodate the character portrayed by her co-star, Errol Flynn, it was retitled for the screen *The Private Lives of Elizabeth and Essex* (1939). Davis knew Flynn lacked the proper training and

THE OLD MAID (1939). As aged Charlotte Lovell

experience required for Essex, and she fought vainly to get Laurence Olivier for the role. In the hands of Michael Curtiz, a director well experienced at handling Flynn as well as Davis, *The Private Lives of Elizabeth and Essex* now seems a long and wordy historical piece, enlivened by Davis's fiery performance.

To be convincing as the middle-aged Elizabeth, thirty-one-year-old Bette Davis courageously sacrificed her appearance beyond the call of duty. Her hairline was shaved back three inches to accommodate the Queen's carrot-colored wigs, and her eyebrows were completely removed to be replaced by thinly penciled lines. Her features were covered by a pasty white make-

THE PRIVATE LIVES OF ELIZABETH AND ESSEX (1939). As Queen Elizabeth I

up base, her lips were made to seem thinner, and pouches were drawn under her eyes. For the role Davis pitched her voice lower than normal, which, in the thirties, was considerably higher than the alto tones she is now known for.

While admiring the film's handsome production values, photographed in Technicolor, the critics deplored the fact that Davis's strong, rich realization of Elizabeth was not matched by a male counterpart worthy of portraying Essex. Flynn was clearly outmatched by Davis, who pulled out all stops to play the aging queen who smashes mirrors so as not to gaze upon her ugly image, rants wildly against her power-hungry lover ("He never wanted me! He wanted my kingdom!"), and mourns when she is forced to send him to his death ("My heart goes to

THE MIRACLE (1938). A role she never played: the young novice

the grave with him"). Nobody else in the large cast had a chance to flesh out a genuine character, not Flynn and certainly not Olivia de Havilland in the pallid role of Elizabeth's lady-in-waiting, Penelope Gray.

This was Bette Davis's first encounter with the color cameras. Had Warners' production plans gone according to schedule, she would have made her Technicolor debut the previous year in their proposed film version of *The Miracle*, under the direction of fabled Max Reinhardt. Tests were made and still portraits were taken. But there were script problems, and the rights had to be cleared. Finally the project was abandoned.

In the forties films that we now dismiss as soap operas commanded more respect. To this extent many of Davis's best films could now be dismissed as "women's pictures," once considered an important and respected genre on the production slate of every major Hollywood studio. Bette Davis thinks that movie-making will eventually reverse its cycle and will swing away from the sex and violence of recent years to accommodate the neglected part of its audience that now prefers to stay away from overly explicit film fare.

By contemporary standards *All This and Heaven Too* (1940) is a period soap opera. Its story of an impossible (and impossibly platonic) love affair, based on an actual scandal that had rocked mid-nineteenth century France, reflects the censorship restrictions of Hollywood in 1940, and Davis bemoans the fact that in her era they had no recourse to a tastefully adult freedom of expression. She is certain that the true-life Henriette Desportes, the demure, long-suffering governess she depicted in that film, actually had a much more intimate relationship with her married employer, the Duc de Praslin (Charles Boyer). Again Anatole Litvak directed a handsome costume drama, from Casey Robinson's screenplay of Rachel Field's popular novel, and drew a restrained and moving performance from Bette Davis, warmly matched by Boyer. His death scene, in which he confesses to loving Henriette "with every drop of blood" in him, is beautifully handled. Due to its meticulous production and the skill and authority of its performances, *All This and Heaven Too* is nearly as rewarding today as it was over three decades ago. Davis says that this reflects her constant battles for the best scripts, supporting casts, and technicians. In those years at Warners she was the queen of the lot, and any important female role had to be turned down by her before studio contractees like Olivia de Havilland, Ida Lupino, or Ann Sheridan could expect a chance at it.

Bette Davis's other 1940 release, *The Letter*, is a strong and haunting film, containing one of her finest performances. Originally a London success with Gladys Cooper, then a Broadway vehicle for Katharine Cornell, Somerset Maugham's play was first filmed by Paramount in 1929 with the legendary Jeanne Eagels. For Warners' remake Davis was reunited with William Wyler, a prospect which pleased her immensely. As it developed, Wyler's conception of her role did not always concur with hers, and following one altercation, Davis admits she walked off the set—something she had never done before. However, she completely credits Wyler for *The Letter*'s success and states in her book, "I lost a battle, but I lost it to a genius. So many directors were such weak sisters that I would have to take over. Uncreative, unsure of themselves, frightened to fight back, they offered me none of the security that this tyrant did."

The setting is Malaya. Leslie Crosbie, the coolly calculating wife of a rubber plantation manager (Herbert Marshall), shoots

THE LETTER (1940). With Herbert Marshall

THE GREAT LIE (1941). With Mary Astor

her lover and fabricates a web of lies to protect herself. Her husband believes her; her counsel (James Stephenson) does not. To save her neck Leslie is forced to pay the dead man's Eurasian wife (Gale Sondergaard) ten thousand dollars to get back an incriminating letter she sent the deceased on the night she killed him. Under Wyler's direction their confrontation scene is memorable, performed without dialogue, yet underscored by the ominous tinkle of wind chimes. The murder trial ends in an acquittal for Leslie, but her husband learns the truth when he discovers his life's savings have been spent to suppress evidence. Cruelly flaunting her infidelity, Leslie rejects her husband's forgiveness shouting: "With all my heart, I still love the man I killed!" Unable to live with her conscience, she walks out into the night shadows, where she knows her lover's widow waits to stab her.

The Letter represents an amalgam of expert craftsmanship, from Wyler's strong, deliberate guidance of the compact Howard Koch screenplay to Tony Gaudio's cunning blend of exotic mood lighting and atmospheric camera images that captured the steamy and faintly sinister setting of rustling leaves and moonlight. And—always enforcing the emotional undercurrents of the plot—Max Steiner's score, largely supported by a two-note "fate" theme.

Davis was brilliant as Leslie, conveying the undercurrent of passion and hysteria lurking in this repressed woman as she tells her lying story of her lover's death or pleads with her lawyer (James Stephenson) to buy the incriminating letter, or finally confessing her feelings about her murdered lover ("Even my agony was a kind of joy!"). James Stephenson is also fine as the lawyer Stephen Joyce, carefully suppressing his loathing for Leslie with the muted comment, "I don't want you to tell me anything except what is needed to save your neck."

For *The Letter*, among the top money-making films of 1940, Bette Davis won her fourth Oscar nomination. But she lost the award to Ginger Rogers, who had made an impressive transition from musicals to drama in *Kitty Foyle*.

Following her labors in *The Private Lives of Elizabeth and Essex* the previous year, Davis had returned to New England for a much-needed rest. In Sugar Hill, New Hampshire, she had met Arthur Farnsworth, assistant manager of Puckett's Inn, where she had been a guest. They found that they had much in common, and their friendship grew and endured beyond her vacation from Hollywood. On New Year's Eve of 1941 they were married. Farnsworth's former experience as a flier helped secure him a job with the Minneapolis Honeywell Company, in charge of Disney training films made for the Air Force.

Early in 1941 Bette Davis briefly served as the only woman ever elected President of the Academy of Motion Picture Arts and Sciences. When she tried to institute some much-needed improvements in the voting procedures, there was so much opposition that she resigned, ignoring threats that she would be professionally blacklisted.

In *The Great Lie*, her first film of 1941, Davis and Mary Astor distinguished a hard-breathing soap opera about two ladies, one noble (Davis) and one wicked (Astor), in love with the same man (George Brent again), who share an elaborate lie about a child's parentage. Originally, the "other woman" role was a shadowy background figure, threatening the romance of Davis and Brent. When Davis ran Astor's test, she not only saw to it that Astor got the role but worked with the actress to rewrite the script in an effort to save a potentially bad film. In the process (and Astor gives Davis all the credit) the distaff roles became of equal importance. So highly did Davis respect her co-star's talent that she allowed Astor to steal the picture with a performance of such brilliance that she easily won 1941's Best Supporting Actress Oscar. Mary Astor has gone on record as saying that her role became the standout one through Davis's efforts to save an inferior script. The film itself, directed by Edmund Goulding, was merely an exercise in histrionics.

Busy as she was during 1941, Davis found the time for a "good luck" salute to Geraldine Fitzgerald, with whom she had become good friends during *Dark Victory*; she played a bit role in Fitzgerald's *Shining Victory*. According to director Irving Rapper and Davis herself, she appeared on the set in costume and makeup, at first passing for a "character extra." Rapper did not immediately recognize her. When he did, he went along with the gag and allowed her to rehearse the scene. Reportedly, this was never actually photographed, because Jack Warner put his foot down. Davis, he said, was contracted to two Warners films a year, and if she appeared in

SHINING VICTORY (1941). With Hermine Sterler. A scene the public never saw.

Shining Victory—even in a bit—she would be entitled to full salary as well as billing. However, a still of this scene exists, presumably shot as a curiosity piece during rehearsal.

After her succession of heavily dramatic roles, it was decided that Bette Davis—and her public—would welcome a change of pace. The result was a "screwball" comedy, *The Bride Came C.O.D.* (1941), reuniting her with James Cagney for the first time since *Jimmy the Gent* (1934). Davis has little regard for the movie: "We both reached bottom with this one." However, she threw herself into her elo-

ping-heiress role with such professional good sportsmanship, as did Cagney in his familiar frenetic style, that the results were sometimes amusing. The plot was mechanical. About to run off and marry a bandleader (Jack Carson), of whom her father disapproves, wealthy socialite Joan Winfield (Davis) is kidnapped by charter pilot Steve Collins (Cagney), who makes a deal with Winfield to deliver his daughter home unmarried. The plane is forced to land near a desert ghost town, where Joan and Steve battle noisily until, inevitably, they fall in love.

William Keighley's direction

77

THE BRIDE CAME C.O.D. (1941). With James Cagney

kept *The Bride Came C.O.D.* moving at too rapid a pace for anyone to get impatient with its slight plot, and the result was far more entertaining than Davis seems to recall. Though the runaway heiress was virtually obsolete by 1941, Davis manages to give her some semblance of life and extracts a few laughs by falling into a cactus bed, shrieking the lines furnished by Julius and Philip Epstein, and alternately pummeling and embracing Cagney.

She then received $385,000 to star in *The Little Foxes* (1941) for producer Sam Goldwyn at RKO, her first loan-out since *Of Human Bondage* seven years earlier—and the last time she would film outside the Warners lot for the duration of her contract there. In exchange for Davis, Goldwyn let Warners borrow Gary Cooper for *Sergeant York*.

On Broadway, Lillian Hellman's *The Little Foxes* had provided the acting apex of Tallulah Bankhead's career. William Wyler filmed Hellman's adaptation of her stage play with meticulous care, "opening up" the story to accommodate the motion picture medium and utilizing much of the original Broadway cast. Hellman's plot focuses on the Hubbards, a predatory Southern clan consumed by greed and ambition, and ruled over by Regina (Davis), a former Hubbard now married to the submissive Horace Giddens (Herbert Marshall). Horace's poor health brings about the most highly charged scene, a confrontation between the scheming Regina and Horace. Their quarrel precipitates his fatal heart attack when Regina decides to let him die, rather than go upstairs for his medicine.

For once Davis and Wyler disagreed strongly on her interpretation. Against her will, Davis says, she was forced to attend Bankhead's stage performance. She had not wanted to be influenced in this way before starting the picture. Yet once having seen Bankhead, Davis could envision no other plausible approach to the role. But Wyler had another conception of Regina, and his quarrels on the set with Davis were bitter and endless. The results displeased her: "I ended up feeling I had given one of the worst performances of my life. This saddened me, since Regina was a great part, and pleasing Willie Wyler was of such importance always to me."

THE LITTLE FOXES (1941). With Herbert Marshall, Charles Dingle and Carl Benton Reid

THE LITTLE FOXES (1941). As Regina Hubbard Giddens

Though Davis claims that *The Little Foxes* was torture to make, the film proved immensely popular. The critics drew on all their superlatives. *Life* accurately predicted that the Davis drawing power might turn this Goldwyn "prestige" picture into a box-office hit. In *Time* James Agee, fully cognizant of the Davis-Wyler set-to, remarked, "The films' foremost dramatic actress not only acts like Tallulah but looks like her." Bosley Crowther called *The Little Foxes* "the most bitingly sinister picture of the year," adding that "Miss Davis's performance, in the role which Tallulah Bankhead played so brassily on the stage, is abundant with color and mood."

As in *The Letter*, Davis, under Wyler's guidance, seems to play on a very taut, highly-charged level. In the emotional stretches the tensions of her disagreement with her director seem to surface in the most-often-imitated Davis mannerisms: the calculated side glances, the flamboyant nervous gestures and lunging movements. (By contrast Patricia Collinge, brilliantly repeating her stage role as the terrified, alcoholic Birdie, was a model of restraint.) In *The Little Foxes* Orry-Kelly's handsome period costumes provide Davis with the frills and flounces that allow her overmannered moments to become amusing, causing the viewer to forget Regina and study the famed Davis technique. Nevertheless, these moments do not spoil the actress's overall delineation; nor do they detract appreciably from a superior motion picture.

For *The Little Foxes* Bette Davis won still another Academy Award nomination. This time Joan Fontaine won for *Suspicion*, although the cognoscenti insist it was a consolation prize for not winning the previous year in a similar but superior story, *Rebecca*.

Back at Warners, Davis once again fought to play a plum role that she didn't get, despite the fact that she was long acknowledged to be the queen of the Warner lot. (Some called her "the fourth Warner brother," with a nod to her box-office power, as well as to the sound-stage and studio improvements her popularity had made possible at Warners.) The part she now wanted was Cassie Tower, the pathetic child-woman verging on the brink of madness, in *Kings Row*. She and Ida Lupino both coveted the assignment. Cassie wasn't the female lead (Ann Sheridan was ideally cast for that), but it was a plum supporting part whose impact would dominate the movie's first half. But that was long before it became an accepted practice for big-name stars to accept so-called "guest star" or "cameo" roles. Jack Warner assured Davis that Cassie was too small a part for her and that she would merely be "doing box-office duty."

Yet "box-office duty" is surely what Bette Davis performed in the screen transcription of another Broadway hit, George S. Kaufman's and Moss Hart's *The Man Who Came to Dinner* (1941). In that hilarious farce, adapted for the screen by the Epstein brothers with happily few changes, the inimitable Monty Woolley repeated his

THE MAN WHO CAME TO DINNER (1941). With Ann Sheridan
and Monty Woolley

leading stage role of caustic author and raconteur Sheridan Whiteside, who suffers an accident during a lecture tour and is confined to a wheelchair in an Ohio household, where he proceeds to disrupt the menage with his eccentric friends and outrageous acts. The showiest roles went to Woolley and Ann Sheridan, who played Lorraine Sheldon, the witchiest actress of all time, in a marvelous change of pace. Davis has said that her role of Maggie Cutler, Whiteside's put-upon secretary (sporting a simple, tailored wardrobe and severe hairdo) is the one in which she played a character closest to her own private personality. A past mistress at the delivery of witty, pungent dialogue, Davis now played second banana to Woolley, who had the best of the wisecracks. Slightly dated today, *The Man Who Came to Dinner* remains among the funniest comedies of the forties.

Smartly directed by William Keighley, and released during 1941's year-end holidays, the movie earned Bosley Crowther's accolade as "unquestionably the most vicious but hilarious cat-clawing exhibition ever put on the screen." He thought Bette Davis should be handed a palm "for accepting the secondary role of the secretary" and that she deserved another one "for playing it so moderately and well." Still, the film belonged to Woolley, ably assisted by such stalwart performers as Reginald Gardiner, Jimmy Durante, Billie Burke, and especially Mary Wickes as Whiteside's panic-stricken nurse, Miss Preen.

In her autobiography Davis recounts an interesting anecdote about this film. Laura Hope Crews, who had once made life difficult for an ingenue playing summer stock on Cape Cod, was cast in a small role in *The Man Who Came to Dinner*. Davis says she went out of her way to be nice to the elderly actress, now reduced to coaching actors in speech and accepting bit roles when she could find them. In appreciation Miss Crews left Davis a present—a gem-encrusted watch that she still cherishes. The former star's last film role, it was unfortunately cut from the film's release print.

During 1942 Bette Davis continued at the peak of her career in a pair of divergent film roles: Stanley Timberlake, the amoral, conniving Southern girl of *In This Our Life*, and Charlotte Vale, the repressed spinster who finds romance in *Now, Voyager*.

Ellen Glasgow's novel *In This Our Life* had won a Pulitzer Prize. The film adaptation, by Howard Koch (*The Letter*), encountered problems with the Production Code people; the last-minute script changes and character revisions, eliminating an entire subplot and suggestions of incest, may have prevented Davis's character from being believable. As the willful daughter of a once-wealthy Virginia family, Davis ignores her own fiance (George Brent) and steals her sister's husband (Dennis Morgan), who later commits suicide. Meanwhile, her ex-beau has fallen in love with her sister Roy (Olivia de Havilland), and when he spurns Davis, her fury causes her to kill a child in a hit-and-run accident, allowing a black boy to take the blame. But there's the inevitable Hays Office retribution: Stanley is tailed for speeding, tries to elude the law and crashes to her death.

Stanley is a role that Bette Davis could have played with all stops out, and although there are those who think her hammy and overblown, this performance contains enough restraint to suggest that director John Huston—his first after *The Maltese Falcon*—had a hand in keeping her acting somewhat more muted than it might otherwise have been.

Overwrought and unconvinc-

IN THIS OUR LIFE (1942). With Charles Coburn

ing, *In This Our Life* is not a very good film, but it is an interesting one with some strong moments, notably the climactic scene in which Stanley pleads with her dying old uncle (Charles Coburn) to help her escape from the consequences of her nefarious deeds. Davis's scenes with de Havilland are also fascinating, if only as a demonstration of contrasting styles of acting. In *The New York Times* Bosley Crowther suggested that casting Davis as Stanley might be intended to counterbalance her uncharacteristically agreeable role in *The Man Who Came to Dinner*. Re-

calling the excellence of her previous Southerner in *The Little Foxes*, Crowther criticized Davis's mannered acting here, concluding, "Her evil is so theatrical and so completely inexplicable that her eventual demise in an auto accident is the happiest moment in the film." One of her lines in the script ("I'd rather do anything than keep still") set the reviewers to criticizing the actress's constant pacing, squirming, and mannered gestures, likening her movements to St. Vitus' disease. Though it was roundly panned, *In This Our Life* made money for Warners.

There are those who protest loudly when the term "soap opera" is used for a better-than-average motion picture. Yet one of Bette Davis's most memorable performances is the neurotic Cinderella heroine of *Now, Voyager*, without doubt among the finest soap operas ever produced in Hollywood. Casey Robinson fashioned his screenplay from the novel by Olive Higgins Prouty, author of that tear-jerking classic, *Stella Dallas*.

In *Now, Voyager* Davis worked for the first time under the direction of Irving Rapper. A look at Rapper's career proves that he couldn't make a good film from a poor script (*The Gay Sisters, Deception*), but given a screenplay of quality, his work ranks high among the so-called "women's directors."

Bette Davis has called *Now, Voyager* one of her favorite pictures and reports that she was "delighted" with the finished product—one of the few occasions when she could say that. Although Warners owned the property, Davis first learned that Irene Dunne would portray the leading role, on loan to Warner Brothers. In a fury she cornered Jack Warner and convinced him that this excellent role was perfectly suited to *her* talents and that she would not

allow it to go to an outside star. Fortunately, Davis got her way. She says, "There wasn't one of my best pictures I didn't have to fight to get. And once I got this one, it was a constant vigil to preserve the quality of the book as written by Olive Higgins Prouty."

Now, Voyager's plot centers on Charlotte Vale, the unwanted child of a Boston matriarch (Gladys Cooper), whose natural dislike turns her daughter into an unattractive and neurotic spinster, verging on a mental breakdown. Through the help of Dr. Jaquith (Claude Rains), a psychiatrist, Charlotte is almost miraculously rehabilitated and, eventually, transformed into a woman of considerable outward chic, although her inner confidence is less than secure. On an ocean voyage Charlotte meets the charming Jerry Durrence (Paul Henreid), a married man with whom she falls hopelessly in love. After she returns to Boston, the scenes with her mother become worse, and when the old woman dies of a heart attack, Charlotte blames herself, returning to the care of Dr. Jaquith. At his sanitarium she befriends Tina, a mentally depressed child who turns out to be Jerry's unwanted daughter. Charlotte meets Jerry again, but they part

NOW, VOYAGER (1942). With Claude Rains

with her memorable line, "Don't ask for the moon. We have the stars."

Bette Davis claims that the character of Jerry was too weak for Charlotte, and she (Davis) likes to think that Charlotte eventually found happiness with Dr. Jaquith.

Now, Voyager's plot is corny romanticism, ripe with coincidence and Cinderella fantasy. Luckily, Bette Davis can make an audience believe in almost any role she essays, and although her change of appearance here (from matronly hair, dowdy clothes, and frumpy figure to svelte, chicly dressed, artfully made-up, and coiffured) is fantastic in the extreme, the viewer sits with incredulity suspended, willing to accept the near-impossible. The actress's art is such that she compensates for the drastic changes wrought by Perc Westmore and Orry-Kelly, making it painfully evident that Charlotte Vale's exterior modishness has far outstretched the young woman's *inner* adjustments. Nowhere in the film is this better conveyed than in the scene in which the transformed

NOW, VOYAGER (1942). As Charlotte Vale

Charlotte has a bitter and ultimately fatal confrontation with her domineering mother. For the fifth year in succession Bette Davis won an Oscar nomination, losing this time to Greer Garson as the high-minded *Mrs. Miniver*.

Lillian Hellman's anti-fascist play, *Watch on the Rhine*, had been a Broadway success in 1941, and when producer Hal Wallis brought it to the screen for Warners in 1943, he retained three members of the original cast whose performances could not possibly have been bettered —Paul Lukas, Lucile Watson, and George Coulouris. Taking the part that Mady Christians had had on Broadway, Davis says, "Mr. Wallis asked me if I'd play it for name value. But it was not ever my favorite part. I know it was a worthwhile film to make."

As the courageous underground leader who finds that he must confront fascism even in a stately Washington mansion, Lukas never had a better role; it won him that year's Academy Award as Best Actor. Appropriately, Bette Davis, playing his

WATCH ON THE RHINE (1943). With George Coulouris, Paul Lukas and Donald Woods

wife, subordinated her usually colorful personality to the story, which seemed quite stagy under Broadway director - producer Herman Shumlin's guidance. Today *Watch on the Rhine* is too static, too verbose and pedantic in its beware-of-fascism polemic. In 1943 its power was considerable. Davis was restrained, and although the film's best scenes went to Lukas, she had a few good moments as she tells off the Fascist De Brancouis (Coulouris) ("We've seen you in so many houses") or says good-bye to her husband, probably forever.

The actress's most placid marriage ended suddenly that summer when Farnsworth collapsed on Hollywood Boulevard from the aftereffects of a fall he had sustained the previous summer. He lived for twenty-four hours, but never regained consciousness. The autopsy disclosed a blood clot.

Warners now produced a musical called *Thank Your Lucky Stars* (1943), which gave many of their contract players an opportunity to sing and dance in "guest star" roles, as themselves. In a two-piece, brocaded evening gown, Davis half sings, half shouts "They're Either Too Young or Too Old," a lament about the wartime shortage of men, then gets tossed about in a wild jitterbug number that amused her fans for its "stunt" value. No thanks to Bette Davis, the song became a hit. On television this sequence has occasionally been eliminated, leaving only a glimpse of Davis as she leaves the night club after her number.

Davis's third and last 1943 movie, *Old Acquaintance*, reunited her with her old nemesis, Miriam Hopkins, under Vincent Sherman's direction. Once again Davis was the long-suffering good woman and Hopkins the bitch. Davis thinks part of their on-the-set problems derived from Miriam's wanting to play a *sympathetic* role in their two films together. John Van Druten's play had opened on Broadway at the close of 1940, with Jane Cowl and Peggy Wood in the respective Davis and Hopkins roles. A "women's picture" from the start, *Old Acquaintance* spanned some eighteen years in the lives of two literary women, whose friendship survives the passage of time despite

THANK YOUR LUCKY STARS (1943). With Conrad Weidel

OLD ACQUAINTANCE (1943). With John Loder

their romantic and professional rivalry. At the film's close the glamorously graying pair drink a toast to their brittle but enduring relationship.

Much has been written about the scene in which Davis was called upon to shake and slap Hopkins, a prospect which cast, crew, and visitors to the set lined up to watch with relish. As Davis tells it, "We rehearsed this scene for hours—not only her eyes were wandering but so was her body, to every corner of the stage. I finally said 'Miriam! If I have to sit on top of the piano to look into your face for this speech, I will!'" Davis notes that Hopkins received the slap on cue, though she wept with

self-pity—a fact unrecorded by cameras shooting from behind Hopkins' back!

The off-screen battle between these two actresses undoubtedly had much to do with the live-wire effectiveness of their many scenes together. One scene, in which Hopkins bitterly accuses Davis of stealing her ex-husband (John Loder), appeared to generate sparks, as Hopkins's shrill hysteria vies with Davis's cool sophistication for audience attention. Aided by the witty script Van Druten and Lenore Coffee had fashioned from the former's play, the studio emerged with a picture that automatically pulled in the distaff customers. James Agee, writing in the *Nation*, marveled, "The odd thing is that the two ladies and Vincent Sherman, directing, make the whole business look fairly intelligent, detailed and plausible; and that on the screen such trash can seem, even, mature and adventurous."

Released in 1944, *Mr. Skeffington* gave Davis one of her best roles. She played Fanny Trellis, a selfish, vain and frivolous young belle of 1914 New York who marries Jewish financier Job Skeffington (Claude Rains), then grows to hate him. For years she sees other men, but when he is seen in the company of another woman, she divorces Skeffington, allowing him to take their daughter to Europe so that she can be free to pursue the social life she enjoys. Years pass, and Fanny is reunited with her estranged, grown daughter, who informs her that Skeffington has been imprisoned by the Nazis. At the film's end, a now-blind Job comes home to the time-ravaged Fanny, whom he still recalls as the young beauty he married.

The Epstein brothers, Philip and Julius, had fashioned so ab-

OLD ACQUAINTANCE (1943). Rehearsing the big scene with Miriam Hopkins.

MR. SKEFFINGTON (1944). With Claude Rains, Dorothy Peterson, and Robert Shayne

sorbing and detailed a script from the best-selling novel by "Elizabeth" that director Vincent Sherman and a strong cast, including Walter Abel, Richard Waring, and George Coulouris, could hardly go wrong. Running to a lengthy 145 minutes, *Mr. Skeffington* is nevertheless mesmerizing as it moves from gaslit New York society to World War II. A number of scenes, especially the poignant reunion of Job and Fanny at the end of the film, succeeded in rising above the dubious sentiment of a line such as "A woman is beautiful only when she is loved!"

For Davis, Fanny Trellis is a dazzling tour-de-force, perhaps significantly reflected in the fact that in her autobiography she calls the film "*Mrs.* Skeffington." Her gradual maturation and decline remain a monument not only to the acting art but also to the skills of cameraman Ernest Haller and make-up expert Perc Westmore. She displays an amazing range, with speech patterns spanning the light frivolity of a young debutante to the low, whiskey-soaked tones of aged dissipation.

Earlier Davis and John Garfield had helped found the Hollywood Canteen for servicemen, as a West Coast counterpart to Broadway's Stage Door Canteen, which had already been toasted in the 1943 film of that name. Not to be outdone, Warners as-

MR. SKEFFINGTON (1944). As the aged Fanny Trellis Skeffington

HOLLYWOOD CANTEEN (1944). With Jack Carson, Jane Wyman and John Garfield

signed Delmer Daves to write and direct a musical called *Hollywood Canteen*, drawing on so much of Warner Brothers' thespian talent that an ignorant film-goer might have thought that the Canteen was strictly a Warners enterprise. Both Garfield and Davis played themselves, with the latter called upon to explain the Canteen's uses. Critic Howard Barnes wrote in the *New York Herald-Tribune*: "Bette Davis presides over the place with artless and wide-eyed aplomb." All of *Hollywood Canteen*'s profits were allotted to war charities.

With fifty-four motion pic- tures to her credit Bette Davis was now passing the prime of her vintage years. Good films would still come her way, but the best of them would be few and far between. In the forties, competition from other expert actresses was strong in Hollywood. In 1943, a year in which Davis was bypassed in the nominations, the Academy Award for Best Actress went to a newcomer, Jennifer Jones. The following year, Fanny Trellis lost out to Ingrid Bergman's tormented Paula Anton in *Gaslight*. It would take six rough years and another actress's ill fortune to put Bette Davis back on top.

Bette Davis appeared in only one film during 1945, but it is a good one. Directed firmly and scrupulously by Irving Rapper (with whom she had worked so harmoniously on *Now, Voyager*), *The Corn Is Green* remains among the most underrated films of its year.

The part of the middle-aged spinster schoolmistress, Miss Moffat, first portrayed in Britain by Sybil Thorndike, had provided Ethel Barrymore with her last great stage success in 1940. Miss Barrymore was sixty-one when she undertook the role; Bette Davis was thirty-six. It was a difficult undertaking for an actress in her mid-thirties—but one that succeeded.

Emlyn Williams' play had interested Davis enough for her to get Warners to buy the screen rights. Casey Robinson and Frank Cavett adapted the heart-warming drama about a resolute Englishwoman who arrives to teach school in an illiterate Welsh mining village in 1890 and discovers that one rough-hewn miner, Morgan Evans (John Dall), is a gifted, sensitive young man. His future as a candidate for Oxford is nearly ruined when a local girl bears his child, then runs off to marry another man. But Miss Moffat convinces Morgan that his des-

tiny lies at col ... she adopts the child, urging him never to return. In the moving final sequence she tearfully watches him borne off to the railroad station in triumph by his singing friends. "Men of Harlech" is a stirring old Welsh song, and the pathos of that moment, though frankly sentimental, is nevertheless affecting as Rapper guides Davis and Dall through their farewell scene ("You mustn't be clumsy this time," Davis murmurs to herself.)

The role of Miss Moffat offers no opportunities for glamour, neurotic mannerisms, or showy acting. Instead it requires warmth, sympathy, and restraint—and Davis meets its demands with a performance of quiet dignity and compassion, with only a faint hint of the "grande dame" attempting a Barrymore role.

Her initial interest in the moody, inquisitive boy who wants to know "what's behind all them books" becomes delicately shaded with love and pride as she realizes his potential for

THE CORN IS GREEN (1945). With John Dall

achievement. Her scene with Morgan, when he breaks down in tears at being called the "schoolmistress' little dog" and she is forced to tell him what he means to her, is handled with artful finesse by the actress.

While *The Corn Is Green* was in production, Davis met painter William Grant Sherry at a Laguna Beach cocktail party, and after a brief courtship they were married. She refers to their relationship as "stimulating," claiming that Sherry matched her in temperament.

Then, for the first and only time Bette Davis turned producer, with the partial cooperation of Warner Brothers. The vehicle she selected was *A Stolen Life* (1946), a remake of a popular Elisabeth Bergner picture,

filmed in England in 1939. Under the aegis of her A.B.D., Inc., production unit Davis commissioned from scenarist Catherine Turney a slick romantic screenplay that afforded her the opportunity to play her first dual role, as identical twins named Pat and Kate Bosworth. Since Kate was thoughtful and kind, while Pat was ruthless and mean, Bette Davis could now double as her own Miriam Hopkins—and with far less trouble on the set! To play the man for whose affections the two girls compete, Davis hired Glenn Ford, a young actor whose promising career had been cut short by the war.

The plot was ideal for a "women's picture." Kate, an artist, meets Bill (Ford), a handsome young lighthouse inspector on a New England coastal island. When the more vivacious Pat turns up, she succeeds in seducing Bill away from her quieter sister. Pat and Bill are married and Kate finds solace with the roughly attractive Karnok (Dane Clark). Later, while Bill is away, the two girls go sailing and are caught in a storm that sweeps Pat overboard to her death. Her wedding ring comes off in Kate's hand as she tries to save Pat. Kate decides to take Pat's place with Bill and attempt to lead that "stolen" life. But when Bill returns she finds that their relationship is explosive, due to Pat's infidelity. It doesn't take Bill long, of course, to discover that "Pat" is really Kate, leading finally to a happy ending.

A Stolen Life is merely high-gloss soap opera but so well made that it succeeds in being entertaining. Certainly, Curtis Bernhardt's direction contrives to get the best from Miss Turney's script, and his Davis-picked cast (including Charlie Ruggles and Walter Brennan) and Rudi Fehr's expert editing helped create the perfect optical illusion of *two* Bette Davises. Particularly impressive is a scene in which one Davis lights the other's cigarette—with a barely noticeable jerk. With the combined camera work of Sol Polito and Ernest Haller, Davis is perhaps at her most attractive in this film, wearing her hair in the long page-boy bob that has always suited her best.

Despite the critics' unfavorable reaction, *A Stolen Life*

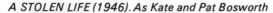

A STOLEN LIFE (1946). As Kate and Pat Bosworth

DECEPTION (1946). With Claude Rains

proved very popular. Davis likes the picture, and although it was to have been the first of five Davis-produced films for Warners, the experience afforded her no more opportunity to actually *produce* than had her previous pictures. Davis says, "I simply meddled as usual. If that was producing, I had been a mogul for years."

For her other 1946 movie, *Deception*, Bette Davis teamed again with her *Now, Voyager* co-stars, Claude Rains and Paul Henreid, and director Irving Rapper. It was an overwrought triangle drama of the classical music world, with Davis as a concert pianist who marries cellist Henreid, her long-lost sweetheart, despite the fact that she has more recently been the mistress of wealthy composer-

conductor Rains. The plot, played as if all three principals were characters in a grand opera, concerns her efforts to keep her past from Henreid, while trying to help his career. Finally, after several pyrotechnic confrontations with the malicious Rains in his impossibly lavish penthouse apartment, she kills him to prevent his telling Henreid the truth about their relationship.

Deception was derived by John Collier from *Jealousy*, a play by Louis Verneuil, filmed once before (1929) with Jeanne Eagels and Fredric March. It undoubtedly marks the one occasion on which a fellow player stole a Davis movie from her; Claude Rains' bravura acting as Alexander Hollenius, the waspish, sardonic composer, usurps the acting honors, despite strong competition from his leading lady. With his shock of white hair and elaborate velvet jacket, he cuts an amusing picture as he quarrels bitterly with Davis while reading the newspaper comics or spews forth his venom at everything and everyone. Davis recently remarked, "The picture wasn't terribly good, but *he* was *brilliant!*" Although Davis had to go through the motions of playing Beethoven's "Appassionata," the piano was actually played by Shura Cherkassky.

On May 1, 1947, shortly after Davis's thirty-ninth birthday, Barbara Davis Sherry was born. The actress was informed that she would not be able to have any more children. With a nod to her eventual four bouts with matrimony, Davis said on a 1971 television "talk" show, "I got a beautiful daughter from one of those awful marriages."

Following the birth of "B.D.," Bette Davis announced that she was considering two scripts: Helen Deutsch's adaptation of Edith Wharton's *Ethan Frome*, and *Women Without Men*, a women's prison story in which she would play opposite Joan Crawford. Both were interesting prospects never realized, although planning on *Ethan*

Frome progressed to the point where two sets were constructed, and costume portraits were taken of Henry Fonda and Margaret Sullavan, who were to have been her co-stars. Irving Rapper would have directed it, with Agnes Moorehead in a supporting role. *Women Without Men* eventually was filmed as *Caged* (1950) with Eleanor Parker and Agnes Moorehead in the parts once set for Crawford and Davis.

Davis was away from the screen a year before returning to begin the ill-advised *Winter Meeting* (1948), and she reports, "The director, Bretaigne Windust, had the idea that he would introduce a brand-new Bette Davis to the screen. He would have been smarter to leave the old one alone."

Winter Meeting, adapted from the novel by Ethel Vance, had a verbose screenplay by Catherine Turney about a neurotic New England poetess who meets a troubled naval hero (James Davis), a younger man, with whom she falls in love. It develops that he had inter ded becoming a priest, but after his war experiences he no longer feels worthy of God. After interminable conversation they part, he with his faith restored and she coming to terms with her father fixation and assorted other

WINTER MEETING (1948). With James Davis

problems.

In one forgettable exchange of dialogue, Mr. Davis says to Miss Davis, "I want to marry you." She replies, "No, you'll rot little by little in small pieces." *Time* magazine jumped upon these lines to comment, "With many more pictures like this, Miss Davis's prestige may suffer the same fate." In *The New York Times* Bosley Crowther blamed screenwriter Turney's script, for which, he wrote, she "should be made to sit through *Winter Meeting* about twenty-five or thirty times." Davis, however, won some of his praise: "She actually catches, at times, some sense of a woman's deep disturbance at a most puzzling turn in an affair of love. And never, let's say to her credit, does she nibble the scenery, as of yore." (Originally, *Winter Meeting* was to have co-starred Burt Lancaster, but he had been wisely discouraged by the script and turned it down.)

Released the same year, *June Bride* provided a welcome bright note amid the heavy downward trend of Davis's career in the late forties. Her first outright comedy in seven years, it teamed her with Robert Montgomery, himself an expert light comedian, in a breezy Ranald MacDougall screenplay, with Bretaigne Windust again assigned to direct. Davis wore a softer hair style, modeled a smart New Look wardrobe, and handled her crisp dialogue in high style.

She played the editor of *Home Life*, a slick women's magazine, who assigns her new assistant (ex-war correspondent Montgomery, who is a former lover) to accompany her on a midwinter assignment, covering an Indiana wedding at a typically middle-class home. During the process of converting the midwinter setting into what looks like an extravagant June wedding, Davis and Montgomery match wits, rekindle their romance, battle some more, and, eventually, get together, only when she tentatively agrees to give up her career for him.

Davis and Montgomery played well together under Windust's brisk direction, and if Davis was not up to Rosalind Russell as a portrayer of a businesslike "boss lady," she seemed relaxed and happy to be enjoying herself. Montgomery's lines, delivered with his usual aplomb, consisted to some degree of comments on

JUNE BRIDE (1948). With Robert Montgomery

101

Davis's coldness: "Even when I was making love to you, I felt you were wondering what time it is."

In 1949 Davis finally hit rock bottom in her years at Warners with *Beyond the Forest*. One advertisement for the film shows her wearing a well-filled blouse and lying back with both hands behind her head, a cigarette dangling from her lips as she gazes up boldly at the slogan "Nobody's as good as Bette when she's bad!" The publicists at Warners must have had tongues well tucked in their cheeks when they devised that one, for Bette Davis is absolutely at her flagrant worst in *Beyond the Forest*.

Davis says she begged Jack Warner not to make her play Rosa Moline ("She's a midnight girl in a nine o'clock town!" screamed Warners' ad copy). She tried to persuade him that she was, at forty, too old and too strong for the character of this modern Madame Bovary who hates her mild doctor-husband (bland Joseph Cotten) and the small Wisconsin mill town they live in, and longs for the excitement of Chicago. The one man (David Brian) that really interests her has money and a hunting lodge, where they carry on a secret affair, but he has no in-tention of marrying her. In order to meet her own selfish needs this ruthless woman commits adultery, abortion, and premeditated murder before contracting peritonitis and expiring beside the railroad tracks, while Max Steiner's noisy and obvious score fuses the strains of "Chicago" with the sound of train engines.

Beyond the Forest is so outrageously bad that it's good—the ultimate example of a perfectly awful picture that's nevertheless quite entertaining. Certainly Bette Davis's extravagant, posturing Rosa is never boring. Based on the Stuart Engstrand novel, Lenore Coffee's script is studded with outlandish lines such as character actor Minor Watson's repeated observation: "You're something for the birds, Rosa! Something for the birds!" In his play *Who's Afraid of Virginia Woolf?* Edward Albee immortalized Rosa's line "What a dump!"—her opinion of the home she shares with Cotten.

Everything about *Beyond the Forest* is lurid, blatant, and totally unbelievable under King Vidor's indulgent direction. Bosley Crowther, in *The New York Times*, deplored the unpleasant grotesqueries of the Davis role and largely blamed Vidor: "Not only has he accepted a thoroughly denigrating script, but he has

BEYOND THE FOREST (1949). With Minor Watson

harshened and uglified Miss Davis so that she's as repulsive as a witch in a cartoon." With an unbecoming black fright wig two feet long, heavy make-up, an atrocious Edith Head wardrobe and perilously high spike heels, Davis staggers about like a third-rate female impersonator. It is a totally unforgettable performance—for all the wrong reasons. This Jezebel was a far cry from her Oscar-winning Julie Marsden.

During the film's production Davis asked for her release from her contract. Jack Warner was taken by surprise, and although he had been considering her for the role of Blanche in *A Streetcar Named Desire*, he agreed. The actress claims that the last line she spoke before leaving the Warners lot was Rosa's appropriate "I can't stand it here anymore!"

Yet later Bette Davis would remark: "I feel very fortunate that Mr. Warner was my boss for eighteen years. Despite our many professional disagreements, I think he ended up with great respect for me, and I hope he thanks me for those seven sound stages that I built at Warners."

After leaving Warner Brothers, Bette Davis and Curtis Bernhardt, who had directed her in *A Stolen Life*, developed a script idea called *The Story of a Divorce*, which they sold to RKO as a Davis vehicle. Bernhardt directed the screenplay that he and Bruce Manning consequently wrote. When the film was released early in 1951, RKO retitled it *Payment on Demand*.

Payment on Demand concerns wealthy, middle-aged Joyce Ramsey (Davis) who faces the failure of her twenty-year marriage to David Ramsey (Barry Sullivan), a highly successful businessman. Recalling the events of their married life, Joyce realizes that it was her ruthless drive and social ambition that ultimately split their union. With the knowledge that David has been seeing another woman (Frances Dee), Joyce threatens to charge him with adultery unless he agrees to meet her substantial financial demands. To avoid a scandal he does so.

On a cruise Joyce meets another divorcee (Jane Cowl), whose life style dismays her, and rejects the attentions of a married man (John Sutton). Joyce and David meet again at their daughter's wedding and afterwards realize that they still love

THE SEESAW YEARS (1950-1960)

each other. As the film ends, their future together looks hopeful.

Ironically, Bette Davis's own marriage was on the rocks at the time she began filming this picture. When Sherry heard rumors that Davis was involved with Barry Sullivan, her leading man, he caused an unpleasant scene at the post-production party, and he and Davis separated. In the ensuing divorce action she won custody of B.D., and Sherry was awarded alimony!

In many facets Joyce Ramsey *is* Bette Davis. Both women are possessed of a drive and ambition too strong for the ordinary man to accommodate; both strive for social equality in a man's world, although both are feminine in manner and fully capable of responding to a husband's affection. Yet Joyce's very strength of character provides the weakening link in her marriage. It is a role which, in many variations, Bette Davis has played over and over, in private life as well as on the screen.

In *Payment on Demand* Davis is ideally cast, responds well to

Bernhardt's direction, and delivers one of her finest performances. In firm control of the part, she succeeds in conveying the pride, vindictiveness, and, ultimately, the lonely despair of a powerful woman whose life is being shattered. Her stunned reaction that her husband wants a divorce, and their climactic scene together with their troubled teenage daughter (Betty Lynn), are played by Davis with her usual professional skill. And she is helped by an intelligent script and a good supporting cast, with the exception of Barry Sullivan who, in the tradition of Davis's leading men, is rather bland as the husband.

PAYMENT ON DEMAND (1951).
With Barry Sullivan

Characteristic of RKO's film-release patterns in those days, *Payment on Demand* was kept on the shelf until after the release of *All About Eve*, which Davis filmed directly afterward. It was then reported by the press that she had signed with RKO to star in John O'Hara's *Appointment in Samarra*, a project that was never realized.

Before *Payment on Demand* was finished, Darryl Zanuck contacted Bette Davis about replacing an ailing Claudette Colbert in *All About Eve*. Colbert had seriously injured her back, and production commitments made it impossible to wait for

her recovery. Zanuck's second choice had been Ingrid Bergman, who declined to return from Italy for the role. His desperate, last-minute choice of Bette Davis was the best thing that could have happened to her career. Among the most scintillating screen comedies ever made, it offered, in Margo Channing, a role so rich in warmth, glamour, humor, and dramatic fireworks that it won her 1950's New York Film Critics Award as Best Actress.

Based on a story by actress-writer Mary Orr, *All About Eve* (1950) drew a large part of its critical and public acclaim from Joseph L. Mankiewicz' brilliant

ALL ABOUT EVE (1950). With Anne Baxter

script and direction and from Bette Davis's bravura perform- ance. In that year's nominations for the Academy Award she faced formidable competition, including a trio of first-rate dra- matic performances (Eleanor Parker in *Caged*, Gloria Swan- son in *Sunset Boulevard*, and her *All About Eve* co-star, Anne Baxter), as well as a comedy characterization so shrewdly timed and performed that it won out over the more solid work of her peers—Judy Holliday in *Born Yesterday*. Nominated for no less than fourteen Oscars, *All About Eve* won six, including one for Best Picture and one for director Mankiewicz.

Margo Channing is a forty- year-old stage star whose life is complicated by Eve Harrington (Baxter), a designing young woman who comes backstage after a performance to profess her great admiration, and man- ages to be hired as Margo's se- cretary-companion. Among the first to suspect Eve of ulterior motives are Margo's outspoken maid Birdie (Thelma Ritter) and drama critic Addison DeWitt (George Sanders), who helps Eve get the job of Margo's under- study. Eve also works her wiles on Lloyd Richards (Hugh Mar- lowe), author of Margo's current hit, and Bill Sampson (Gary Merrill), Margo's director and fiance. Before the film's end Eve has stolen a plum role away from Margo, shaken Richards' mar- riage, and won a coveted acting award. The story ends as it began, only this time it is Eve who appears to be the target for the flattery of another young aspirant (Barbara Bates), perhaps as ruthless as herself.

As Eve, Anne Baxter is so quietly accurate that one tends almost to overlook her next to the astringent perfection that Bette Davis brings to Margo. With an attractive, shoulder-length bob and an appropriately flamboyant style, Davis so well realizes the aura of a larger-than-life theatrical fable that many drew inevitable comparisons between her Margo and Tallulah Bankhead, using as "evidence" the fact that she had played Bankhead's stage roles on the screen in *Dark Victory* and *The Little Foxes*.

Davis manages to dominate every scene in which she appears: in the much-quoted party scene where she makes a magnificent, though tipsy, entrance ("Fasten your seat belts—it's going to be a bumpy evening!"); in her violent quarrel with Bill, where her rage is clearly tempered with fear; and even in her quieter moments where her looks of ironic amusement and self-pity speak volumes. (Watch her in the car scene with Celeste Holm, in which she conveys her longings and regrets, while her friend, in secret shame, knows that she has deliberately ar-

ranged to have Eve take Margo's place at that night's performance.)

Davis has this to say of *All About Eve*: "I can think of no project that from the outset was as rewarding from the first day to the last. It is easy to understand why. It was a great script, had a great director, and a cast of professionals all with parts they liked. It was a charmed production from the word go. After the picture was released, I told Joe he had resurrected me from the dead."

On July 28, 1950, prior to the release of *All About Eve*, Davis married her leading man, Gary Merrill.

In 1951 the newlyweds went to England to co-star in *Another Man's Poison*, a hard-breathing melodrama of murder, suspicion,

ALL ABOUT EVE (1950).
With Gary Merrill, Anne Baxter, and George Sanders

ANOTHER MAN'S POISON (1952). With Emlyn Williams and
Gary Merrill

and vengeance on the Yorkshire moors. Val Guest's talky script was given little help by Irving Rapper's uninspired direction. Davis played Janet Frobisher, a high-strung novelist who kills her blackmailing husband when he threatens to expose her affair with her secretary's fiance (Anthony Steel). Merrill is cast as George Bates, a bank robber fleeing from the police who takes shelter in Janet's gloomy house and becomes her unwilling partner in crime, helping her dispose of Frobisher's body. In subsequent plot complications Janet becomes deranged when Bates shoots her pet horse, Fury, after the animal breaks its leg.

She tries to kill Bates by tampering with his car, but fails. The ending is suitably ironic: Janet poisons Bates, and when a meddling neighbor (Emlyn Williams) informs her that he knows everything, she faints, only to find that she's regained consciousness by drinking the brandy with which she's just poisoned Bates. The film ends with a close-up of her, laughing hysterically.

In its absurd way *Another Man's Poison* is almost as entertaining a bad movie as *Beyond the Forest*. As is often the case when Davis has a poor script, she pulls out all the stops, giving an overly mannered, overly intense performance that holds the viewer's attention, while tickling his funnybone. Perhaps the peak of the film's many overwrought scenes is the one in which Davis discovers the demise of her favorite horse, confronting Merrill with wild eyes and the memorably articulated lines: "You—killed—*Fury!*" and "I used to talk to him every night." In *The New Statesman,* Frank Hauser observed, "It is fascinating watching Bette Davis play everything in a blaze of breathtaking absurdity. From beginning to end, there is not a lifelike inflection, a plausible reaction. No one has ever accused her of failing to rise to a good script; what this film shows is how far she can go to meet a bad one."

Gary Merrill remained under contract to 20th Century-Fox, and when he was cast in the episodic drama, *Phone Call From a Stranger* (1952), Davis took the small role of Marie Hoke, a bedridden invalid, who is visited by David Trask (Merrill), sole survivor of the plane crash that killed her husband (Keenan Wynn). It was the smallest role Davis had played since the start of her career and anticipates the later-accepted tradition of established stars accepting so-called "cameo" roles—supporting parts that offer an opportunity to dominate a scene or two. Several years later, for its television anthology series, *20th Cen-*

PHONE CALL FROM A STRANGER (1952). With Gary Merrill

THE STAR (1952). With Sterling Hayden

tury-Fox Hour, that studio incorporated Davis's footage into a forty-five-minute "remake" of the movie, re-titled *Crack-Up*.

That year Davis also played the role of Margaret Elliott, a Hollywood has-been, in Bert Friedlob's independent production of *The Star*, which Fox released in time to qualify for 1952 Oscars. Originally written for Joan Crawford by the husband-and-wife team of Katherine Albert and Dale Eunson, *The Star* is a cliche-ridden, economy-sized *Sunset Boulevard*, centering on the attempted comeback of a once-great movie actress, a former Oscar winner whose popularity has faded. To live, she is forced to sell her personal ef-

fects, is jailed for drunken driving, makes a ridiculous screen test for a comeback, and finally finds happiness with a sympathetic boat-builder (Sterling Hayden).

Bosley Crowther, comparing Margaret Elliott to Margo Channing in *All About Eve*, wrote in *The New York Times*: "Whether shadowing an auction of her belongings or looking in on the remains of her broken home or tottering blearily through a drunken orgy, Miss Davis is eloquent and sure." *Time* magazine summed up her performance this way: "It is a marathon one-woman show and, all in all, proof that Bette Davis—with her strident voice, nervous stride, mobile hands and popping eyes—is still her own best imitator."

Among Davis's most memorable scenes in *The Star*, two are outstanding, but for entirely different reasons. The first involves Margaret Elliott in a screen test which she ruins by trying to play a middle-aged woman as a sexy siren. Logically, this ex-star, desperate for a return to the screen, would bend over backward to please her director. Instead, of course, she is ridiculous. In scenes like this *The Star* is completely phony, and direc-

tor Stuart Heisler offers Davis no help. However, in her subsequent scene Davis is marvelous: in a studio projection room, Margaret Elliott watches that test in a pathetic scene well described by Crowther: "If ever humiliation and cold, clammy, cantankerous chagrin have been thoroughly acted in a movie, it is done by Miss Davis here."

In competition for the 1952 Oscar, Davis had to contend with Joan Crawford, who had by-passed *The Star* to appear in *Sudden Fear*. Both lost out to film novice Shirley Booth, re-

THE VIRGIN QUEEN (1955). With Herbert Marshall

creating her successful Broadway role in *Come Back, Little Sheba*. Coincidentally, this was a part for which its producer, Hal Wallis, had briefly considered Bette Davis.

Before the release of *The Star* Davis agreed to return to the stage, for the first time in twenty-two years, in a musical revue entitled *Two's Company*. At the time she said: "I felt like a coward not coming back. I've had wonderful offers. I kept turning them down. I felt terrified at the thought of coming back. I had the children (she and Gary Merrill had adopted a girl and a boy), my home, I was lazy. It's too comfortable out there. I have no real feeling of security about myself. That's probably a very healthy thing."

Two's Company presented Davis in musical numbers by Vernon Duke and Ogden Nash, staged by Jerome Robbins: "Turn Me Loose on Broadway," "Roll Along, Sadie," "Purple Rose," and "Just Like a Man." Jules Dassin directed the show's various sketches in which she teamed with comedian Hiram Sherman. On opening night in Detroit it ran over three hours. Davis fainted onstage during her first number, returning to reassure the audience with "You can't say I didn't fall for you."

Poor health plagued her during the show's lengthy out-of-town try out, during which John Murray Anderson performed artistic surgery to save it from folding on tour. On December 15, 1952, Bette Davis made her Broadway bow as a musical comedy star. In the *New York Herald-Tribune* Walter Kerr called her "thoroughly workmanlike" and "magnificently willing," concluding: "Miss Davis unbends so much that there's some doubt in my mind whether she'll ever be able to straighten up again."

Two's Company closed (early in February) after only ninety performances. Bette Davis's health problem had finally proved to be osteomyelitis of the jaw, forcing her to leave the show and undergo a serious operation, followed by six weeks in the hospital and a long recuperation at home. She and Gary Merrill bought a rambling old house near Portland, Maine, and retreated there.

Davis feels that her career was seriously damaged at that time when the syndicated columnist Walter Winchell reported erroneously that she had cancer of the jaw. Threatened with a lawsuit, Winchell published a retraction but the major damage had been done.

Davis says that it was two

years after the operation before she felt fully recovered. Three years after leaving *Two's Company* she was lured back to Hollywood by 20th Century-Fox with a script entitled *Sir Walter Raleigh* in which she would again play Queen Elizabeth, this time opposite Richard Todd as Raleigh. To get Bette Davis back Darryl Zanuck had the script rewritten to enlarge her role and changed the film's title to *The Virgin Queen* (1955). In a subsequent *New York Times* interview with Howard Thompson, Davis expressed great enthusiasm for the Harry Brown-Mindred Lord script and her first experience with the CinemaScope cameras. To play Elizabeth, Davis allowed her head to be shaved, so that she could accurately depict the aging monarch, whose famed red wigs made little effort to disguise her tonsorial misfortunes.

The Virgin Queen is simplified history, handsomely produced, efficiently directed by Henry Koster, and very well acted. (Her one-time co-star Herbert Marshall, now playing supporting roles, appeared as Lord Leicester.) Playing opposite a sturdier actor than Errol Flynn and less inclined to dominate the proceedings with extravagant acting, Davis cut a

STORM CENTER (1956).
With Paul Kelly

convincing, if grotesque, picture of the queen's thirst for power and her sexual frustrations. Her scene with the ambitious Raleigh, in which he pleads for ships to sail to the New World, succeeds in striking sparks lacking in the earlier film on Elizabeth.

In April 1955, before the release of *The Virgin Queen*, Davis appeared at the annual Academy Awards ceremony to hand Marlon Brando his Oscar for *On the Waterfront*. Over her shaven head she wore Elizabeth's starched nightcap—and won a prolonged ovation.

Early in 1956 she made her television debut in a pair of dramatic shows and starred in two

113

films: *Storm Center*, a Phoenix Production released through Columbia, and her first Metro-Goldwyn-Mayer film, *The Catered Affair*.

Storm Center is, to date, the only motion picture directed by Oscar-winning screenwriter Daniel Taradash (*From Here to Eternity*). The script Taradash co-authored with Elick Moll concerns Alicia Hull (Davis), a widowed librarian who stands up to civic pressure to remove a book on Communism from her shelves. As a result she herself is branded as subversive and is replaced by her assistant (Kim Hunter). Upset and confused, young Freddie Slater (Kevin Coughlin), whose reading habits Alicia had guided, sets fire to the library and destroys it. The townspeople then come to realize the error of their prejudices, and they ask Alicia to return and help them rebuild the library.

For years *The Library* (as it had originally been known) had been mentioned for production, most often as a possible comeback for Mary Pickford, who had retired from the screen in 1933, following *Secrets*. Davis gave a good performance as the dedicated librarian, but the story's melodramatic turns of plot detracted from the plausibility of so serious a theme. In *The New York Times* Bosley Crowther expressed more appreciation for the film's thesis than for its treatment. Of the star he wrote, "Miss Davis makes the prim but stalwart lady human and credible," and he praised her "fearless and forceful performance." The film fared poorly at the box office.

The Catered Affair, made after *Storm Center* but released ahead of it, was Gore Vidal's adaptation of an original teleplay by Paddy Chayefsky. It dealt with an average Bronx family (Davis, Ernest Borgnine, Debbie Reynolds), caught up in a very human situation: the mismanagement of the daughter's wedding. Following the realistic style of other Chayefsky plays (*Marty, The Bachelor Party*), it had "little people" acting out their small and often poignant crises before arriving at reasonable, if not altogether happy, solutions. The leading players, including Barry Fitzgerald as the family uncle, were given "arias" to perform before the cameras.

Under Richard Brooks's direction this curious film works well at moments, but Davis is clearly miscast as the forlorn but game Bronx housewife. Stuffed with padding, wearing dowdy clothing, sensible shoes, and an unbecoming, frumpy wig, she takes a stab at a role originally played to perfection on television by Thelma Ritter. But most of the time it is simply Bette Davis play-acting—or the star slumming.

In 1957 Bette Davis was unable to find a movie script that satisfied her. Instead she performed in several television dramas. At the time she said: "I still work for money. I won't starve if I don't work, nor will I die on the vine. But I think it wiser to stay in touch with my chosen profession." When not working, she and Gary Merrill spent time with their children in their Maine retreat.

Davis reported being intrigued at seeing her old films on television: "I like it. I see no reason to feel shame. It's kind of fascinating to be able to sit back and, in a sense, see the beginning, the middle and the career at its height. As for some of the bad ones we made as babies, it's possible to sit home and get angered."

In August 1958 *Film Daily* reported that Davis was in Venice with Martine Carol, Vittorio de Sica, Jacques Sernas and Martita Hunt, working under the direction of Alberto Cavalcanti in a comedy called *Les Noces Venitiennes* (*Venetian Weddings*). No such film was

THE CATERED AFFAIR (1956).
With Debbie Reynolds

ever released.

Bette Davis continued to appear on television. After portraying a strong but doomed pioneer woman in a segment of the *Wagon Train* series, she said, "The tragedy is we can't sit around and wait for good things. We have to take whatever comes along. I've done many TV shows I didn't want to do, just to keep busy. Any of us would be delighted to make movies again, if there were any to do. Unfortunately, this is the age of mediocrity in show business."

Her comments were reflected in the two films in which she appeared during 1959, *John Paul Jones* and *The Scapegoat*. In the former, a ponderous and expen-

JOHN PAUL JONES (1959).
As Catherine the Great

sive spectacle directed by John Farrow and starring Robert Stack in the title role, she accepted the brief "guest star" part of Catherine the Great. Forced to mouth some inane lines, she was unable to summon up even a modicum of her artistry. The film was roundly criticized for discarding historical accuracy and substituting lavishly staged sea battles. Sadly, it was John Farrow's last film.

The next film, *The Scapegoat*, held more promise, but the results were disappointing. Based on a novel by Daphne Du Maurier, it had a screenplay credited to its director, Robert Hamer, and was co-produced by Miss Du Maurier in association with its star, Alec Guinness. Guinness undertook the dual role of a British professor and his lookalike, a French count, whose identity he assumes. Davis portrayed the latter's bedridden, morphine-addicted mother, a cigar-smoking old harridan attired in lace and ostrich plumes. Although accorded co-star billing with Guinness, Bette Davis has surprisingly little footage. This has been partially explained by the actress herself: "When I made *The Scapegoat* with Alec Guinness, he cut my part into such shreds that my appearance in the final product made no sense at all. This is an actor who plays by himself, unto himself. In this particular picture he plays a dual role, so at least he was able to play with himself."

During the autumn of 1959 Davis and Merrill toured across the country in *The World of Carl Sandburg*. *Life* magazine reported: "Using excerpts from the poet's stories, songs, verses and jokes, the team puts on a breezy, poetic vaudeville which shows off Sandburg at his best."

On July 6, 1960, Bette Davis was awarded a divorce from Gary Merrill. The charge was

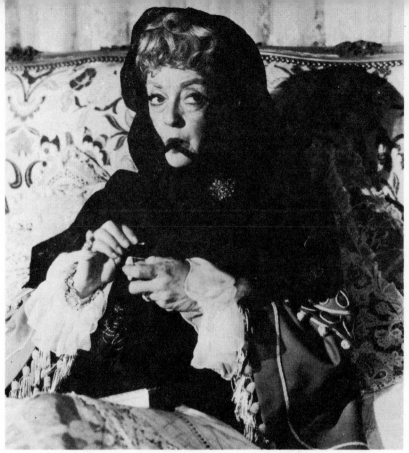

THE SCAPEGOAT (1959). As the Countess

"cruel and abusive treatment," since it was said that the actor's frequent and unexplained absences from their home had had an adverse effect upon his wife and children.

That September Davis brought *The World of Carl Sandburg* to Broadway, with Leif Erickson replacing Gary Merrill. The show had done very well on the road, but the New York notices were not good, and the production closed after only twenty-nine performances. Davis reports that it was "a bitter blow." That winter she and the children stayed in New York. She began work on her autobiography to pass the time while she searched for a film or play worth doing.

117

In 1961 Bette Davis's mother died at the age of seventy-six. The actress claims that she "would have been nothing" without Ruthie's vitality, her brutal honesty, her wisdom, joy, and "guts." She says that she and Bobby suddenly felt like orphans. They had the tombstone inscribed: "RUTHIE—you will always be in the front row."

In the spring of 1961 Davis was back before the cameras, acting in *Pocketful of Miracles*. To date, this sentimental comedy marks the last film work of veteran director Frank Capra, who had already filmed the Damon Runyon tale in 1933 as *Lady for a Day*, when May Robson had starred as Apple Annie. In this Cinderella role of an elderly Broadway peddler, who sells apples and likes her gin, Davis was reunited with her co-star from *A Stolen Life*, Glenn Ford, who played a Manhattan bootlegger named Dave the Dude. Her street-corner cronies don't know it, but Annie has a daughter, Louise (Ann-Margret), who has been brought up in a Spanish convent and thinks her mother is the wealthy socialite Mrs. E. Worthington Manville. The plot thickens when Louise writes her mother that she is engaged to a Spanish nobleman and is bringing him and his fa-

THE FIRST LADY OF FRIGHT (1961-1965)

ther across to meet her. On Annie's behalf, all of her friends rally around and turn her into a veritable grande dame, complete with penthouse apartment. The hoax works; Louise and her fiance are royally received and return to Spain none the wiser. Annie is happy but out of her milieu, and she goes back to selling apples.

United Artists released the picture in time for the 1961 year-end holidays. *Pocketful of Miracles* is dated hokum, but its fairy-tale plot is so entertainingly told by screenwriters Hal Kantor and Frank Tugend, producer-director Capra, and a fine cast of mostly veteran actors (including Thomas Mitchell, Edward Everett Horton, and Peter Falk) that audiences were willing to suspend disbelief and exit humming the movie's popular title song, written by Sammy Cahn and James Van Heusen.

In an interview with Hollywood writer Joe Hyams during the making of this film, Davis said, "This role is fun, but a lot of work. It's a hard kind of character because I have so much going for me with this appearance (ragged wardrobe, gray wig, heavy eyebrows, weather-beaten complexion). I don't want to overdo it, and it is a hard line to draw."

The public made *Pocketful of Miracles* far more popular than the critics had anticipated. A welcome relief in a movie season rife with sex and violence, the film offered audiences two Bette Davises: one of such harridan proportions that one critic compared her to a character in a Charles Addams cartoon; the other, a beautiful dowager who spoke and behaved so well that one could scarcely be expected to believe that this was still Broadway's Apple Annie.

Directly on the heels of this film's release Bette Davis returned to Broadway as Maxine Faulk in Tennessee Williams's *The Night of the Iguana.* In a red wig, jeans, and man's shirt unbuttoned to an alarming depth, Davis played what critic Henry Hewes in the *Saturday Review* described as "a coarse, middle-aged Gorgon." It was a role that Williams wanted her to play, and although Maxine was not the best part, Davis says, "I would rather have the third part in a Tennessee Williams play than a lead in an ordinary play."

As Maxine, the owner of a

POCKETFUL OF MIRACLES
(1961). With Peter Falk and
Glenn Ford

run-down Mexican hotel, Davis was required to bring earthy comfort to a deteriorating, defrocked priest, played by Patrick O'Neal. It was a flamboyant role, and despite differences with director Frank Corsaro, Davis made a striking impression. However, Margaret Leighton, as a much more typical Williams character—a lonely, sensitive woman saddled with a dying old father—had the best role and played it with such finesse that she won that season's Antoinette Perry ("Tony") Award.

Six months later Shelley Winters replaced Bette Davis in the play. Davis had good reason

POCKETFUL OF MIRACLES
(1961). As "Mrs. E.
Worthington Manville"

for leaving—an offer to play the role of Jane Hudson in *What Ever Happened to Baby Jane?* A grotesque horror yarn with a Hollywood background, this film opened the door to a new Davis career—as the star of lurid horror films, the female equivalent of Vincent Price, who had been frightening audiences for years in ghoulish roles. Many of Davis's contemporaries have declined to accept such parts, preferring either to stay in retirement or to await that rare, suitable role in what has become an increasingly male-dominated story market. But Bette Davis is a professional movie actress, and retirement doesn't appeal to her; she would rather play demented

old ladies, monster mothers, and elderly bank robbers in the medium she knows best—films.

What Ever Happened to Baby Jane? (1962) was the first—and the best—of these roles for Davis. Producer-director Robert Aldrich had signed Joan Crawford to co-star but had had difficulty interesting a studio in what many considered a doubtful project, with two "has-been" stars. Released by Warner Brothers, the film was an immediate success—and the surprise movie "sleeper" of the year. It rejuvenated both the Crawford and Davis careers and sent each into a round of subsequent thrillers, albeit of lesser quality. For Davis, Jane Hudson offered so fascinating an excursion into the grotesque that she met the challenge with a flair that won her her tenth Oscar nomination. Crawford, in a somewhat less strenuous although equally difficult part, was bypassed in the nominations.

Lukas Heller's screenplay and Robert Aldrich's direction work together to rivet the audiences' attention with shock effects and startling twists of plot. The setting is an old Hollywood mansion, where the reclusive Hudson sisters, Blanche (Crawford) and Jane (Davis), lead a strange existence. Pre-credit flashbacks in-

120

form us that both were rival film stars of another era: Jane a golden-haired youngster whose star and talent faded as she matured, at the same time that Blanche's success and popularity increased. Then, at the height of her career, Blanche suffered a crippling automobile accident for which Jane is blamed. Forced to care for her crippled sister, the unbalanced Jane learns that Blanche plans to sell their house and put her in a home, and she sets out to take revenge, at the same time that she plans a comeback, bizarrely dressed as she was when a child star. Her revenge takes hideous and ultimately murderous forms, until she brings about her sister's near-death and her own descent into total madness.

Whiskey-voiced, slovenly, grotesquely gowned and made up, Davis played Jane Hudson as a figure out of some Grand Guignol nightmare. Alternately funny and frightening, and sometimes both, she croaked a simpering version of one of her old movie songs, "I'm Writing a Letter to Daddy," flirted ludicrously with a bewildered, mother-ridden pianist (Victor Buono), and worked assiduously to reduce her sister to a pitiful wreck. Her final scene, in which she danced raptly on a crowded

WHAT EVER HAPPENED TO BABY JANE? (1961). With Joan Crawford

beach beside the emaciated body of her sister, was genuinely moving. The performance was not great acting, but a bravura turn by an actress who knew exactly what she was doing.

The critics received the film with mingled outrage and admiration. Critic Andrew Sarris offered the best comment: "The casting is inspired. Poor Joan Crawford trapped upstairs in her wheelchair and menaced by crazy Bette Davis downstairs—the screen's eternal masochist confronting the screen's eternal sadist. What could be more fitting for what most reviewers have dismissed as an old-fashioned gaslit melodrama?"

In September of 1962, before

121

WHEN EVER HAPPENED TO BABY JANE? (1961). As Jane Hudson

the release of *What Ever Happened to Baby Jane?*, Davis tried a publicity stunt that received widespread attention. She advertised herself in the movie trade publications: "MOTHER OF THREE—10, 11 AND 15—DIVORCEE. AMERICAN. THIRTY YEARS EXPERIENCE AS AN ACTRESS IN MOTION PICTURES. MOBILE STILL, AND MORE AFFABLE THAN RUMOR WOULD HAVE IT. WANTS STEADY EMPLOYMENT IN HOLLYWOOD (HAS HAD BROADWAY).

BETTE DAVIS, C/O MARTIN BAUM, GAC. REFERENCES UPON REQUEST."
By way of explanation Davis said at the time: "I was just flinging down the gauntlet to the bankers who wouldn't finance a picture with me in it. Some of the great things I wanted to do were turned down by bankers because no picture of record in the past ten years with me in it had made money. I wanted everybody to know I was back in Hollywood—and back with a vengeance! This is my town. I've always loved it and still do. It was a great town once, and it can be again."

Among the resulting offers which Davis chose not to accept were a Las Vegas production of *Bye, Bye, Birdie*, and a cameo role as a madam in Frank Sinatra's *4 for Texas*. But she did play a lady attorney on the *Perry Mason* television series.

Davis returned to Hollywood filmmaking in the 1964 *Dead Ringer*, filmed at Warners under the direction of Paul Henreid, a favorite co-star from the old days. Once again she played identical twins, in a latter-day variation on *A Stolen Life*. This time one twin kills the other, after many years of separation, in revenge for stealing away her fiance. Poor working Bette then assumes the role of wealthy widow Bette—and finds that she has her late sister's suspicious lover (Peter Lawford) in the bargain. *Dead Ringer*'s subsequent plot twists are hardly worth detailing, although they do offer

Davis an interesting tour de force. Rian James's novel, *Dead Pigeon*, had already provided the plot for a 1946 Dolores Del Rio vehicle, *La Otra*, filmed in Mexico.

Dead Ringer was a lurid and unconvincing melodrama, though Davis, photographed by her favorite Warners cameraman, Ernest Haller, tries to galvanize the film with her trade marked assortment of eye-popping, body-twitching mannerisms. *(The New York Times* called it "sheer cinematic personality on a rampage.") But no amount of the Davis relish for a tour-de-force role could keep the film from being absurd. (To further emulate the old Davis films at Warners, Andre Previn even wrote a noisy Max Steiner-like score, to no avail.)

Davis then went to Rome for the film version of Alberto Moravia's novel *La Noia (Boredom)*, retitled *The Empty Canvas* (1964) for English-speaking countries. The film was directed in so haphazard and improvisational a style by Damiano Damiani that Davis, upon her return to the United States, had few kind words for Italian production methods. She preferred, she said, the completed scripts and more professional working conditions of the Hollywood and

DEAD RINGER (1964). As Edith Phillips

London film studios. When questioned by a reporter as to why she had agreed to make *The Empty Canvas*, she replied, "There just aren't that many good women's roles around any more—most of the top parts now are being written for men. But we'll be back when the cycle is completed."

In *The Empty Canvas,* Davis plays the wealthy American mother of Horst Buchholz, a struggling young Roman artist who enters into an affair with his model (Catherine Spaak) that threatens to destroy him. Obsessed with her, he can neither persuade her to become his wife

*DEAD RINGER (1964). As
Edith Phillips and Margaret de Lorca*

who received special "Miss Bette Davis" billing, played her part so far beyond the hilt that she became entertainingly ludicrous. A blonde Buster Brown wig and thickly-laid-on Southern drawl heightened the amusement. In *The New York Times*, Howard Thompson, likening her to a Pekingese, thought she supplied the movie's comedy relief: "At one point, for instance, she presides at dinner like a cobra as she watches Mr. Buchholz paw a servant. Even funnier is her saucer-eyed discovery of the two people in her bedroom." (Spaak and Buchholz are caught making love in Davis's bed.)

Neither this film nor *Dead Ringer* did very well at the box office, but her third 1964 release, the film version of Harold Robbins's popular best-seller, *Where Love Has Gone*, fared much better. It was a story that bore more than a few similarities to the real-life case of a movie star's daughter involved in the murder of her mother's lover. (In the Robbins version the celebrity is now a famed lady sculptor.) Davis played the supporting role of Mrs. Gerald Hayden, a well-groomed, domineering San Francisco socialite and mother of the trouble-plagued heroine (Susan Hayward). Her scenes consisted largely of heated, vitriolic ex-

nor discourage her nymphomaniac tendencies. Eventually she runs away with another man, and the artist shows signs of benefiting, creatively, from the whole affair.

Faced with another inferior script (such as this was), Davis, changes with the daughter whose life she has controlled and, in a sense, destroyed. Edward Dmytryk directed a script by John Michael Hayes that offered a typical Robbins mixture of sex, sentiment, and melodrama. Though Davis appeared to be giving the role all of her old verve and authority, she later referred to this film as one of the "stinking pieces of crap" that she made just for the money. *Where Love Has Gone*, she reports, "paid for my daughter's wedding."

In 1965 Davis returned to the horror genre, signing with Robert Aldrich to re-team with Joan Crawford for a follow-up to *What Ever Happened to Baby Jane?* This one, a Gothic melodrama called *Hush . . . Hush, Sweet Charlotte* was obviously designed to equal the thrills—and financial success—of its predecessor. After production was started, there were rumblings of trouble between the two stars, and Crawford was reported ill. On two occasions the production was temporarily suspended; then Crawford contracted virus pneumonia and had to be replaced. Aldrich offered the role to Vivien Leigh and Loretta Young, but neither wanted to play in a horror film. Then Davis insisted he get her old friend Olivia de Ha-

LA NOIA (THE EMPTY CANVAS) (1964). As Dino's mother

villand. He did so, and de Havilland's portrait of calculated sweetness, covering a basic malevolence, offers a superb counterpoint to the distraught madness of Davis's haggard, outlandishly dressed character.

The plot is more Grand Guignol ghoulishness. In an old Louisiana mansion, aging Charlotte Hollis (Davis) leads a reclusive life with her slatternly housekeeper, Velma (Agnes Moorehead). When her decaying home is threatened by demolition for a new highway, Charlotte sends for her cousin Miriam (de Havilland). Thirty-seven years earlier,

WHERE LOVE HAS GONE (1964). With Susan Hayward

Charlotte's married lover had been horribly murdered and mutilated during a lavish party, causing her withdrawal into madness. Now, with Miriam's visit, the family skeletons begin to rattle, horrible memories recur with the appearance of a severed hand, a disembodied head, weird piano music—and additional violence. The culprit is revealed as Miriam, in collusion with the family doctor (Joseph Cotten). As preposterous as Davis's previous film with Aldrich, *Hush . . . Hush, Sweet Charlotte* is almost equally bizarre and entertaining. Both are based on novels by Henry Farrell, only this time Farrell joined Lukas Heller in writing the screenplay.

Again Davis had an actress's field day, closely equaled by a scene-stealing Agnes Moorehead as a whining, snarling servant, and a subtly evil Olivia de Havilland. Davis even won some praise, being singled out by *Time* for her handling of the climactic scene in which she is confronted by an apparition seemingly returned from the grave: "Sobbing, she crawls to the top of the steps, sees something, freezes like a psychotic spaniel, then goes howling down backward and sideways, all matted curls, eyeballs and quivering flesh. By the time she rumbles to a stop, audiences may justly wonder which apparition is scarier—Bette at the bottom or that Thing up top with muddy feet."

Davis had long admired Bri-

126

HUSH . . . HUSH, SWEET CHARLOTTE (1964). With Olivia de Havilland

tain and the British, and was pleased to return there in 1965 for the title role in *The Nanny*, directed for Hammer Films by Seth Holt. This time she played a dowdy character far more sane, sensible—and indeed repressed—than in her previous bouts with the thriller genre. Much of Jimmy Sangster's script (from a novel by Evelyn Piper) proceeds so smoothly and calmly that the audience is certain that Davis, as a British nanny suspected by her young charge of having murdered his infant sister, must eventually turn to murder and mayhem. The cat-and-mouse game between the nanny and the boy is played with mounting tension and a few moments of genuine horror, as when the nanny calmly and serenely refuses to help the woman dying of a heart attack in front of her. For Davis, the role of the nanny was a comparatively restrained exercise after years of outlandish excess.

THE NANNY (1965).With William Dix

127

During 1966 Bette Davis suffered the career frustrations of an aging but still vital actress whom some thought had lost her box-office draw. She has admitted that one of the biggest disappointments of her career was not getting the role of Martha in the movie version of *Who's Afraid of Virginia Woolf?*, for which Elizabeth Taylor won her second Academy Award. Another setback was losing Maxine Faulk to Ava Gardner when *The Night of the Iguana* was filmed. Later her name was mentioned for *The Killing of Sister George*, but director Robert Aldrich ultimately decided to have Beryl Reid repeat her stage performance.

Davis turned down twenty-five thousand dollars to play a one-day role as Paul Newman's mother in *Cool Hand Luke*, a part that went to Jo Van Fleet. Davis felt that the size of the role would not have been commensurate with her billing and that the public would feel cheated. Instead she returned to England and another starring part for Hammer Films in *The Anniversary*. She was joined by a cast that had played in the London stage version of the story, to be directed by Alvin Rakoff, a young Canadian television director with no major films to his credit. Rakoff and Davis failed

RECENT YEARS (1966-1972)

to agree on her interpretation, and she had him replaced with veteran producer-director Roy Ward Baker.

The Anniversary is hardly a horror film, although Mrs. Taggart, the character portrayed by Davis, is without doubt one of the champion monster-mothers of all time. The story centers on that lady's wedding anniversary, which she has continued to celebrate since her husband's welcomed demise a decade earlier. A stylish, waspish woman of wealth, Mrs. Taggart had, in her way, managed to keep her three grown sons attached to her apron strings—a situation she has no intention of allowing anyone to change. At this year's celebration matters come to a head, and eventually mama is left alone but undefeated, convinced that she'll have them all back with her for next year's party.

Wearing an eye patch and punctuating her often funny dialogue with bursts of derisive laughter, Davis plays the hideous harridan with obvious relish. She frightens her youngest son's fiancee by placing a glass

THE ANNIVERSARY (1968).
As Mrs. Taggart

variously announced that Tammy Grimes, Eleanor Parker, and even Bette Davis might replace her. Instead Susan Hayward came out of semiretirement to do so. Davis made no more films until she returned to England in the spring of 1969 to play opposite Michael Redgrave in *Connecting Rooms*. Directed by Franklin Gollings, it was a drama about some unfortunate souls living in a seedy Bayswater boarding house. Davis played a cellist who befriends Redgrave, a schoolmaster unfairly accused of misconduct with a student. Their elderly romance is complicated by her jealous young protege, Mickey (Alexis Kanner), a would-be songwriter who spitefully reveals the older man's secret. In the end the cellist and the former teacher walk off together—past a poster heralding a play starring Margo Channing!

eye under her pillow, protects her fetish-minded older son, and in general appears to be deriving a ribald enjoyment from the havoc she is wreaking. Soon after making this film Davis told an interviewer, "It may not be the greatest movie ever made, but it's a good old-fashioned Bette Davis movie and I *do* get the best of everybody in the end. And it was a challenge."

In 1967 Davis continued to perform on occasional television shows. When Judy Garland failed to fulfill contractual requirements as Helen Lawson in *Valley of the Dolls*, Fox reported that she had "withdrawn for personal reasons," and

In Britain, *Connecting Rooms* was held back two years before its release; in the United States aside from a few trade showings that created little interest, it has not been seen. American television may be its next destination. The English critics found little to rave about. The British Film Institute's *Monthly Film Bulletin* called it "another doomed attempt to locate an old-fashioned, melodramatic romance in a

129

CONNECTING ROOMS (1971). With Alexis Kanner

contrived, contemporary setting."

In 1970, Davis appeared on
television as a former jewel thief
opposite Robert Wagner in an
episode of *It Takes a Thief*. Then
she signed with American International for a film eventually released as *Bunny O'Hare*, in
which she played a grandmother
who joins with an ex-thief (Ernest Borgnine) to become a mo-
torcycling, hippie-clad pair of
Robin Hood bank-robbers, "lib-
erating" the money for worthwhile causes. Davis said afterward, "It was my first all-on-
location film and it was hell!"

Of the movie, she said at the
time, "It's an intelligent script,
it's funny, there's lots in it that's
sweet and nice, and it has a lot
to say in its mild little way."
Several months later, after view-
ing the release print, she repu-
diated the film and sued American International for over five
million dollars. She charged
them with "fraudulent misrepre-
sentation," claiming that she
had signed for "a social com-
mentary with humorous under-
tones," but that added footage
and indiscriminate editing had
made of the film "a tastelessly
and inarticulately assembled

slapstick production." In her suit, Davis was completely supported by director Gerd Oswald, who stated, "I feel that they mutilated the picture completely after I turned in my final cut. They made a different film from that which we had conceived."

The critics seemed to agree with Davis and Oswald. In *The New York Times,* Vincent Canby called the movie "a silly, foolishly entertaining movie that may well disappear before anyone else sees it. Miss Davis, however, gives a performance that may be one of the funniest and most legitimate of her career, which has been spectacular for mannerisms that overwhelmed every character she's ever played, with the notable exceptions of Leslie Crosbie (*The Letter*), Regina Giddens (*The Little Foxes*), and Margo Channing (*All About Eve*)."

Since *Bunny O'Hare,* Bette Davis has continued to go where the work is. With no intention or wish to retire, she willingly travels where there's a role for an older actress. She has filmed a pilot for a prospective television series about a Margo Channing-like interior decorator—which has never been shown to the public. And in the spring of 1971 she and British actress Anne Heywood signed to co-star in a movie that was never made—*And Presumed Dead,* a kidnap thriller, to have been filmed in

BUNNY O'HARE (1971). With Ernest Borgnine

MADAME SIN (1972). With Denholm Elliott

Switzerland. However, on the eve of production, producer Albert Selden failed to raise the money.

During 1971 Davis *did* film two television movies, *Madame Sin* and *The Judge and Jake Wyler*. The former premiered on American television in January 1972 and is being shown outside of the United States as a theatrical movie. Admittedly the most expensive movie ever made for television, it was written especially for Davis by Barry Orringer and David Greene and directed by Greene for executive producer Robert Wagner, who also co-starred. In a black wig, exotic jewelry, and bizarre

make-up, the actress appears as a female Fu Manchu who somewhat resembles Gale Sondergaard in *The Letter*. Davis says she enjoyed playing this larger-than-life villainess. The movie was shot on location in Scotland, and although it was rumored to be the pilot film for a possible series, the results left much to be desired. In the British film magazine *Films and Filming*, Julian Fox wrote, "As played by Bette Davis, she has her moments, chief among them the classic delivery of leaden lines which on Miss Davis's lips take on a Wildean ring. Otherwise, she is reduced by the limitations of the script to a meticulously orating

THE JUDGE AND JAKE WYLER
(1972). As Judge Meredith

gargoyle. As a further inroad into the tragically crumbling structure of Miss Davis's former reputation, blame should be apportioned equally between the cynicism of the film's producers (Julian Wintle and Lou Morheim) and Miss Davis's own unflagging compliance."

The Judge and Jake Wyler, filmed for Universal television at the close of the year, presents Davis as the retired, hypochondriac Judge Meredith, who runs a detective agency with a pair of former convicts. In the spring of 1972, she went to Rome for a role in support of Alberto Sordi and Silvana Mangano in Luigi Comencini's *Lo Scopone Scientifico* (*The Scientific Cardplayer*).

Few of Bette Davis's contem-

poraries are still active in show business. Joan Crawford has found it easier to promote Pepsi-Cola than locate a good script; Ida Lupino prefers directing to performing; Olivia de Havilland occasionally plays a featured role in ill-advised movies such as *The Adventurers* and *Pope Joan*; Myrna Loy, Barbara Stanwyck, and Joan Bennett appear in television movies.

Bette Davis concludes, "I'll never make the mistake of saying I'm retired. You do that, and you're finished. You just have to make sure you play older and older parts. Hell, I could do a million of those character roles. But I'm stubborn about playing the lead. I'd like to go out with my name above the title."

It is easy to believe that this tough, strong-minded actress will, in fact, go out with her name "above the title." For four decades she has weathered all trends (and created a few), followed her own direction in her own mettlesome way, and rewarded filmgoers with a host of dazzling, often larger-than-life performances. From the nervous, odd-mannered blonde of the early thirties to the outspoken lady of today, she has created a unique personality that remains indelible in the hearts and minds of filmgoers.

BIBLIOGRAPHY

Arliss, George *My Ten Years in the Studios.* Little, Brown & Co., Boston, 1940.

Astor, Mary. *A Life on Film.* Delacorte Press, New York, 1971.

Baxter, John. *Hollywood in the Thirties.* A.S. Barnes & Co., New York, 1968.

Davis, Bette. *The Lonely Life.* G.P. Putnam's Sons, New York, 1962.

Gow, Gordon. *Hollywood in the Fifties.* A.S. Barnes & Co., New York, 1971.

Hewes, Henry (ed.) *The Best Plays of 1961-1962.* Dodd, Mead & Co., New York, 1962.

Higham, Charles and Greenberg, Joel. *Hollywood in the Forties.* A.S. Barnes & Co., New York, 1968.

Kronenberger, Louis (ed.). *The Best Plays of 1952-1953.* Dodd, Mead & Co., New York, 1954.

———.*The Best Plays of 1960-1961.* Dodd, Mead & Co., New York, 1961.

McClelland, Doug. *The Unkindest Cuts.* A.S. Barnes & Co., Cranbury, New Jersey, 1972.

Mantle, Burns (ed.). *The Best Plays of 1928-1929.* Dodd, Mead & Co., New York, 1929.

———.*The Best Plays of 1929-1930.* Dodd, Mead & Co., New York, 1930.

———.*The Best Plays of 1930-1931.* Dodd, Mead & Co., New York, 1931.

Noble, Peter. *Bette Davis.* Skelton Robinson, London, 1947.

Osborne, Robert. *Academy Awards Illustrated.* Ernest E. Schwork, La Habra, California, 1969.

Ringgold, Gene. *The Films of Bette Davis.* The Citadel Press, New York, 1966.

Shipman, David. *The Great Movie Stars.* Crown Publishers, New York, 1970.

HONORS AND AWARDS

1935—*Dangerous*—Academy Award
1938—*Jezebel*—Academy Award
1939—*Dark Victory*—Academy Award nomination
1940—*The Letter*—Academy Award nomination
1941—*The Little Foxes*—Academy Award nomination
1942—*Now, Voyager*—Academy Award nomination
1944—*Mr. Skeffington*—Academy Award nomination
1950—*All About Eve*—New York Film Critics Award and
Academy Award nomination
1952—*The Star*—Academy Award nomination
1962—*What Ever Happened to Baby Jane?*
—Academy Award nomination

THE FILMS OF BETTE DAVIS

The director's name follows the release date. A (c) following the release date indicates that the film was in color. Sp indicates Screenplay and b/o indicates based/on.

1. BAD SISTER. Univ., 1931. *Hobart Henley.* Sp: Raymond L. Schrock & Tom Reed, b/o story by Booth Tarkington. Cast: Conrad Nagel, Sidney Fox, ZaSu Pitts, Slim Summerville, Humphrey Bogart, Charles Winninger, Emma Dunn. Small-town girl falls in love with confidence man. BD played her sensible sister.

2. SEED. Univ., 1931. *John M. Stahl.* Sp: Gladys Lehman, b/o novel by Charles G. Norris. Cast: John Boles, Genevieve Tobin, Lois Wilson, Raymond Hackett, ZaSu Pitts. Drama about novelist and his family. BD played small role as his daughter.

3. WATERLOO BRIDGE. Univ., 1931. *James Whale.* Sp: Benn W. Levy, b/o play by Robert E. Sherwood. Cast: Mae Clarke, Kent Douglass (Douglass Montgomery), Doris Lloyd, Ethel Griffies. First film version of Sherwood play, remade by MGM in 1940 and 1956, when retitled *Gaby.* BD played sister of ill-fated heroine's lover.

4. WAY BACK HOME. Radio, 1932. *William A. Seiter.* Sp: Jane Murfin. Cast: Phillips Lord, Effie Palmer, Mrs. Phillips Lord, Frank Albertson, Dorothy Peterson, Frankie Darro. Drama about Maine preacher, originally released as *Other People's Business.* BD played heroine.

5. THE MENACE. Col., 1932. *Roy William Neill.* Sp: Dorothy Howell & Charles Logue, b/o novel by Edgar Wallace. Cast: H. B. Warner, Walter Byron, Natalie Moorhead, Halliwell Hobbes. Murder melodrama, with BD as heroine.

6. HELL'S HOUSE. Capital, 1932. *Howard Higgin.* Sp: Paul Gangelin & B. Harrison Orkow, b/o story by Howard Higgins. Cast: Junior Durkin, Pat O'Brien, Junior Coughlan, Charley Grapewin, Emma Dunn. Innocent teenager is falsely sent to reformatory. BD played his girl friend. Also released as *Juvenile Court.*

7. THE MAN WHO PLAYED GOD. WB, 1932. *John Adolfi.* Sp: Julian Josephson & Maude Howell, b/o story by Gouverneur Morris & play by Jules Eckert Goodman. Cast: George Arliss, Violet Heming, Ivan Simpson, Louise Closser Hale, Donald Cook, Ray(mond) Milland, Hedda Hopper. Musician becomes deaf, turns anonymous philanthropist. BD had ingenue lead, her first important role. Dorothy Malone played the role in WB's 1955 remake, *Sincerely Yours.*

8. SO BIG. WB, 1932. *William A. Wellman.* Sp: J. Grubb Alexander & Robert Lord, b/o novel by Edna Ferber. Cast: Barbara Stanwyck, George Brent, Dickie Moore, Guy Kibbee, Hardie Albright, Alan Hale, Elizabeth Patterson. Farm woman sacrifices for her son. BD played artist in love with him. Phyllis Haver played role in FN's 1924 version, and Nancy Olson in WB's 1953 remake.

9. THE RICH ARE ALWAYS WITH US. WB, 1932. *Alfred E. Green.* Sp: Austin Parker, b/o novel by E. Pettit. Cast: Ruth Chatterton, George Brent, Adrienne Dore, John Miljan, Mae Madison. BD as young socialite hopelessly infatuated with newspaper correspondent GB, who loves divorcee RC.

10. THE DARK HORSE. WB, 1932. *Alfred E. Green.* Sp: Joseph Jackson & Wilson Mizner, b/o story by Melville Grossman, Joseph Jackson & Courtenay Terrett. Cast: Warren William, Guy Kibbee, Frank McHugh, Vivienne Osborne, Sam Hardy, Robert Warwick. BD was a Progressive Party worker in love with campaign manager WW.

11. CABIN IN THE COTTON. WB, 1932. *Michael Curtiz*. Sp: Paul Green, b/o novel by Harry Harrison Kroll. Cast: Richard Barthelmess, Dorothy Jordan, Henry B. Walthall, Hardie Albright, Tully Marshall, Berton Churchill. Sharecropper's son tries to better himself. In her first "bad girl" role, BD played the local siren.

12. THREE ON A MATCH. WB, 1932. *Mervyn LeRoy*. Sp: Lucien Hubbard, b/o story by Kubec Glasmon & John Bright. Cast: Ann Dvorak, Joan Blondell, Warren William, Grant Mitchell, Lyle Talbot, Glenda Farrell, Humphrey Bogart, Patricia Ellis, Jack LaRue, Edward Arnold, Allen Jenkins. Three schoolgirls renew their acquaintance. BD was the scholarly one; now a stenographer. Marie Wilson played the role in WB's 1938 remake, *Broadway Musketeers.*

13. 20,000 YEARS IN SING SING. WB, 1933. *Michael Curtiz*. Sp: Wilson Mizner & Brown Holmes, b/o book by Lewis E. Lawes. Cast: Spencer Tracy, Arthur Byron, Lyle Talbot, Sheila Terry, Louis Calhern. BD as the loyal girl friend of mobster/convict ST. Ann Sheridan played the role in WB's 1940 remake, *Castle on the Hudson.*

14. PARACHUTE JUMPER. WB, 1933. *Alfred E. Green*. Sp: John Francis Larkin, b/o story by Rian James. Cast: Douglas Fairbanks, Jr., Leo Carrillo, Frank McHugh, Claire Dodd. BD was an unemployed stenographer involved with a dope smuggler and two pilots.

15. THE WORKING MAN. WB, 1933. *John Adolfi*. Sp: Maude T. Howell & Charles Kenyon, b/o story by Edgar Franklin. Cast: George Arliss, Hardie Albright, Theodore Newton, Gordon Westcott, J. Farrell MacDonald, Douglas Dumbrille. Manufacturer GA saved BD's rival firm from failure and fostered her romance with his nephew, HA.

16. EX-LADY. WB, 1933. *Robert Florey*. Sp: David Boehm, b/o story by Edith Fitzgerald & Robert Riskin. Cast: Gene Raymond, Frank McHugh, Monroe Owsley, Claire Dodd, Kay Strozzi. BD was a commercial artist who favored free love over marriage.

17. BUREAU OF MISSING PERSONS. WB, 1933. *Roy Del Ruth.* Sp: Robert Presnell, b/o book by John H. Ayres & Carol Bird. Cast: Lewis Stone, Pat O'Brien, Glenda Farrell, Allen Jenkins, Ruth Donnelly, Hugh Herbert, Alan Dinehart, Marjorie Gateson, Adrian Morris, Henry Kolker. BD was a mystery woman falsely accused of killing her husband.

18. FASHIONS OF 1934. WB, 1934. *William Dieterle.* Sp: F. Hugh Herbert, Gene Markey, Kathryn Scola & Carl Erickson, b/o story by Harry Collins & Warren Duff. Cast: William Powell, Frank McHugh, Verree Teasdale, Reginald Owen, Henry O'Neill, Phillip Reed, Hugh Herbert, Nella Walker, Dorothy Burgess, Jane Darwell. Con man WP and fashion artist BD teamed to steal the latest designs from Paris.

19. THE BIG SHAKEDOWN. WB, 1934. *John Francis Dillon.* Sp: Niven Busch & Rian James, b/o story by Sam Engels. Cast: Charles Farrell, Ricardo Cortez, Glenda Farrell, Allen Jenkins, Henry O'Neill. BD was a druggist's wife who nearly died in childbirth when given phony drugs.

20. JIMMY THE GENT. WB, 1934. *Michael Curtiz.* Sp: Bertram Milhauser, b/o story by Laird Doyle & Ray Nazarro. Cast: James Cagney, Alice White, Allen Jenkins, Arthur Hohl, Alan Dinehart, Phillip Reed, Hobart Cavanaugh, Mayo Methot, Jane Darwell. BD was reluctantly wooed and won by con man JC.

21. FOG OVER FRISCO. WB, 1934. *William Dieterle.* Sp: Robert N. Lee & Eugene Solow, b/o story by George Dyer. Cast: Donald Woods, Margaret Lindsay, Lyle Talbot, Arthur Byron, Hugh Herbert, Douglas Dumbrille, Robert Barrat, Henry O'Neill, Irving Pichel, Alan Hale, William Demarest. Bored socialite BD consorted with gangsters and was murdered.

22. OF HUMAN BONDAGE. RKO, 1934. *John Cromwell.* Sp: Lester Cohen, b/o novel by W. Somerset Maugham. Cast: Leslie Howard, Frances Dee, Kay Johnson, Reginald Denny, Alan Hale, Reginald Owen. Crippled medical student LH was obsessed with cockney tramp BD. Her first great role, still considered among her best. Remade by WB in 1946 with Eleanor Parker and by MGM in 1964 with Kim Novak.

23. HOUSEWIFE. WB, 1934. *Alfred E. Green.* Sp: Manuel Seff & Lillie Hayward, b/o story by Robert Lord & Lillie Hayward. Cast: George Brent, Ann Dvorak, John Halliday, Ruth Donnelly, Hobart Cavanaugh, Robert Barrat. Copywriter BD encouraged the attentions of married ex-boyfriend GB.

24. BORDERTOWN. WB, 1935. *Archie Mayo.* Sp: Laird Doyle & Wallace Smith, b/o novel by Carroll Graham. Cast: Paul Muni, Margaret Lindsay, Gavin Gordon, Arthur Stone, Robert Barrat, Eugene Pallette, Hobart Cavanaugh, Henry O'Neill. Unhappily married, BD fell for Mexican attorney PM, killed her husband and went insane. Ida Lupino played the role in WB's partial remake *They Drive By Night* (1941).

25. THE GIRL FROM 10TH AVENUE. WB, 1935. *Alfred E. Green.* Sp: Charles Kenyon, b/o play by Hubert Henry Davies. Cast: Ian Hunter, Colin Clive, Alison Skipworth, John Eldredge, Phillip Reed, Katherine Alexander, Mary Treen. Poor girl BD reformed and married drunken playboy IH.

26. FRONT PAGE WOMAN. WB, 1935. *Michael Curtiz.* Sp: Roy Chanslor, Lillie Hayward, & Laird Doyle, b/o story by Richard Macaulay. Cast: George Brent, June Martel, Dorothy Dare, Joseph Crehan, Winifred Shaw, Roscoe Karns, J. Carroll Naish. Engaged to rival reporter GB, BD proved her skill by solving murder.

27. SPECIAL AGENT. WB, 1935. *William Keighley.* Sp: Laird Doyle & Abem Finkel, b/o idea by Martin Mooney. Cast: George Brent, Ricardo Cortez, Jack LaRue, Joseph Crehan, J. Carroll Naish, Joseph Sawyer, Irving Pichel, Robert Barrat, Paul Guilfoyle. Syndicate secretary BD helped agent GB get evidence against her racketeering boss, RC.

28. DANGEROUS. WB, 1935. *Alfred E. Green.* Sp: Laird Doyle. Cast: Franchot Tone, Margaret Lindsay, Alison Skipworth, John Eldredge, Dick Foran. BD won her first Oscar as a has-been stage star, downed by alcohol but reformed by architect FT.

29. THE PETRIFIED FOREST. WB, 1936. *Archie Mayo.* Sp: Charles Kenyon & Delmer Daves, b/o play by Robert E. Sher-

wood. Cast: Leslie Howard, Genevieve Tobin, Dick Foran, Humphrey Bogart, Joseph Sawyer, Porter Hall, Charley Grapewin, Paul Harvey. BD was unhappy waitress in desert cafe attracted to itinerant poet LH. Jean Sullivan played the role in WB's 1943 remake, *Escape in the Desert*.

30. THE GOLDEN ARROW. WB, 1936. *Alfred E. Green.* Sp: Charles Kenyon, b/o play by Michael Arlen. Cast: George Brent, Eugene Pallette, Dick Foran, Carol Hughes, Craig Reynolds, Ivan Lebedeff, Catherine Doucet, Henry O'Neill, Hobart Cavanaugh, Bess Flowers. Restaurant cashier BD impersonated an heiress for publicity campaign.

31. SATAN MET A LADY. WB, 1936. *William Dieterle.* Sp: Brown Holmes, b/o novel by Dashiell Hammett. Cast: Warren William, Alison Skipworth, Arthur Treacher, Winifred Shaw, Marie Wilson, Porter Hall. Private-eye WW is led astray by mystery woman BD hunting for an art treasure. The story was filmed twice by WB as *The Maltese Falcon:* in 1931 with Bebe Daniels, in 1941 with Mary Astor. Today Davis still calls this by its in-production title, *The Man in the Black Hat.*

32. MARKED WOMAN. WB, 1937. *Lloyd Bacon.* Sp: Robert Rossen & Abem Finkel. Cast: Humphrey Bogart, Eduardo Ciannelli, Jane Bryan, Lola Lane, Mayo Methot, Isabel Jewell, Rosalind Marquis, Henry O'Neill, Allen Jenkins, John Litel. BD was a clip-joint hostess who testified against her racketeer boss, EC.

33. KID GALAHAD. WB, 1937. *Michael Curtiz.* Sp: Seton I. Miller, b/o novel by Francis Wallace. Cast: Edward G. Robinson, Humphrey Bogart, Wayne Morris, William Haade, Jane Bryan, Harry Carey, Veda Ann Borg, Joyce Compton. Crooked fight promoter EGR finds his mistress BD attracted to his top fighter WM. Shown on TV as *The Battling Bellhop* to avoid confusion with UA's 1963 remake, in which Lola Albright played the BD role. Sylvia Sidney played it in WB's altered 1941 remake, *The Wagons Roll at Night.*

34. THAT CERTAIN WOMAN. WB, 1937. *Edmund Goulding.* Sp: Edmund Goulding. Cast: Henry Fonda, Ian Hunter, Anita Louise, Donald Crisp, Katherine Alexander, Mary Phillips, Minor

Watson, Sidney Toler. Gangster's widow BD becomes secretary, marries weakling, and finds happiness elusive. A remake of UA's *The Trespasser* (1929), with Gloria Swanson.

35. IT'S LOVE I'M AFTER. WB, 1937. *Archie Mayo*. Sp: Casey Robinson, b/o story by Maurice Hanline. Cast: Leslie Howard, Olivia de Havilland, Patric Knowles, Eric Blore, George Barbier, Spring Byington, Bonita Granville, E. E. Clive, Veda Ann Borg. BD and LH were a temperamental acting team involved with stagestruck heiress OD.

36. JEZEBEL. WB, 1938. *William Wyler*. Sp: Clement Ripley, Abem Finkel & John Huston, b/o play by Owen Davis, Sr. Cast: Henry Fonda, George Brent, Donald Crisp, Fay Bainter, Margaret Lindsay, Henry O'Neill, John Litel, Gordon Oliver, Spring Byington, Richard Cromwell. BD won her second Oscar as a willful New Orleans belle who loses her man and gains humility. FB won a supporting Oscar.

37. THE SISTERS. WB, 1938. *Anatole Litvak*. Sp: Milton Krims, b/o novel by Myron Brinig. Cast: Errol Flynn, Anita Louise, Ian Hunter, Donald Crisp, Beulah Bondi, Jane Bryan, Alan Hale, Dick Foran, Henry Travers, Patric Knowles, Lee Patrick, Laura Hope Crews, Harry Davenport, Paul Harvey, Mayo Methot. Small-town girl BD marries reckless reporter EF and endures the San Francisco earthquake.

38. DARK VICTORY. WB, 1939. *Edmund Goulding*. Sp: Casey Robinson, b/o play by George Emerson Brewer, Jr., and Bertram Block. Cast: George Brent, Geraldine Fitzgerald, Humphrey Bogart, Ronald Reagan, Henry Travers, Cora Witherspoon, Dorothy Peterson, Virginia Brissac. BD had her favorite role as a headstrong heiress dying of a brain tumor. Remade by UA as *Stolen Hours* (1963), with Susan Hayward.

39. JUAREZ. WB, 1939. *William Dieterle*. Sp: John Huston, Aeneas MacKenzie, & Wolfgang Reinhardt, b/o play by Franz Werfel and book by Bertita Harding. Cast: Paul Muni, Brian Aherne, Claude Rains, John Garfield, Donald Crisp, Joseph Calleia, Gale Sondergaard, Gilbert Roland, Henry O'Neill, Harry Davenport, Louis Calhern. BD was the doomed Empress

Carlotta.

40. THE OLD MAID. WB, 1939. *Edmund Goulding.* Sp: Casey Robinson, b/o play by Zoë Akins, adapted from novel by Edith Wharton. Cast: Miriam Hopkins, George Brent, Donald Crisp, Jane Bryan, Louise Fazenda, James Stephenson, Jerome Cowan, William Lundigan. BD was an unwed mother whose daughter grew up thinking she was her old maid aunt.

41. THE PRIVATE LIVES OF ELIZABETH AND ESSEX. WB, 1939. (c) *Michael Curtiz.* Sp: Norman Reilly Raine & Aeneas MacKenzie, b/o play by Maxwell Anderson. Cast: Errol Flynn, Olivia de Havilland, Donald Crisp, Vincent Price, Alan Hale, Henry Stephenson, Henry Daniell, Leo G. Carroll, Nanette Fabares (Fabray), John Sutton, Doris Lloyd, Ralph Forbes, Robert Warwick. BD was Good Queen Bess. Alternate TV title: *Elizabeth the Queen.*

42. ALL THIS AND HEAVEN TOO. WB, 1940. *Anatole Litvak.* Sp: Casey Robinson, b/o novel by Rachel Field. Cast: Charles Boyer, Jeffrey Lynn, Barbara O'Neil, Virginia Weidler, Helen Westley, Walter Hampden, Henry Daniell, Harry Davenport, George Coulouris, Montagu Love, Janet Beecher, June Lockhart, Richard Nichols, Ann E. Todd. BD was governess in the household of French nobleman CB and his neurotic wife, and later involved in the wife's murder. Based on the real-life, unsolved "Case of Mlle. D."

43. THE LETTER. WB, 1940. *William Wyler.* Sp: Howard Koch, b/o play by W. Somerset Maugham. Cast: Herbert Marshall, James Stephenson, Frieda Inescort, Gale Sondergaard, Bruce Lester, Cecil Kellaway, Doris Lloyd, (Victor) Sen Yung. BD shot her lover and contrived with her lawyer to prove her "innocence." A remake of Par.'s 1929 film with Jeanne Eagels. In 1947 WB released an altered remake, *The Unfaithful,* with Ann Sheridan.

44. THE GREAT LIE. WB, 1941. *Edmund Goulding.* Sp: Lenore Coffee, b/o novel by Polan Banks. Cast: George Brent, Mary Astor, Lucile Watson, Hattie McDaniel, Grant Mitchell, Jerome Cowan, Thurston Hall, Russell Hicks, Doris Lloyd. Heiress BD married GB and fought to adopt his child by MA. MA won a sup-

porting Oscar.

45. THE BRIDE CAME C.O.D. WB, 1941. *William Keighley.* Sp: Julius J. & Philip G. Epstein, b/o story by Kenneth Earl & M. M. Musselman. Cast: James Cagney, Stuart Erwin, Jack Carson, George Tobias, Harry Davenport, Eugene Pallette, William Frawley, Edward Brophy. BD's wealthy father arranged to have flier kidnap her on the eve of her elopement.

46. THE LITTLE FOXES. RKO, 1941. *William Wyler.* Sp: Lillian Hellman, from her stage play. Cast: Herbert Marshall, Teresa Wright, Richard Carlson, Patricia Collinge, Dan Duryea, Charles Dingle, Carl Benton Reid. BD joined her greedy brothers in a lucrative business deal, ultimately committed murder.

47. THE MAN WHO CAME TO DINNER. WB, 1941. *William Keighley.* Sp: Julius J. & Philip G. Epstein, b/o play by George S. Kaufman & Moss Hart. Cast: Ann Sheridan, Monty Woolley, Richard Travis, Jimmy Durante, Reginald Gardiner, Billie Burke, Elisabeth Fraser, Grant Mitchell, Mary Wickes, George Barbier, Ruth Vivian, Charles Drake, Russell Arms, John Ridgely. Conniving MW meddled in the romance of his secretary (BD) and a newspaper editor (RT).

48. IN THIS OUR LIFE. WB, 1942. *John Huston.* Sp: Howard Koch, b/o novel by Ellen Glasgow. Cast: Olivia de Havilland, George Brent, Dennis Morgan, Charles Coburn, Frank Craven, Billie Burke, Hattie McDaniel, Lee Patrick, Ernest Anderson. Selfish BD stole her sister's husband, drove him to suicide, accidentally killed a child, and died in an auto crash.

49. NOW, VOYAGER. WB, 1942. *Irving Rapper.* Sp: Casey Robinson, b/o novel by Olive Higgins Prouty. Cast: Paul Henreid, Claude Rains, Gladys Cooper, Bonita Granville, Ilka Chase, John Loder, Lee Patrick, Franklin Pangborn, Katherine Alexander, Mary Wickes. BD was a mother-dominated ugly duckling who found romance on a cruise and mental health in a sanitarium.

50. WATCH ON THE RHINE. WB, 1943. *Herman Shumlin.* Sp: Dashiell Hammett, b/o play by Lillian Hellman. Cast: Paul Lukas, Geraldine Fitzgerald, Lucile Watson, Beulah Bondi,

George Coulouris, Donald Woods, Henry Daniell, Donald Buka. BD was the wife of anti-Nazi German PL, forced to kill blackmailing GC.

51. THANK YOUR LUCKY STARS. WB, 1943. *David Butler.* Sp: Norman Panama, Melvin Frank, & James V. Kern, b/o story by Everett Freeman & Arthur Schwartz. Cast: Dennis Morgan, Joan Leslie, Edward Everett Horton, S.Z. Sakall, Ruth Donnelly, Joyce Reynolds. Guest Stars: Humphrey Bogart, Eddie Cantor, Olivia de Havilland, Errol Flynn, John Garfield, Ida Lupino, Ann Sheridan, Dinah Shore, Alexis Smith, Jack Carson, Alan Hale, George Tobias, Hattie McDaniel, Spike Jones. As herself, BD sang and danced "They're Either Too Young or Too Old."

52. OLD ACQUAINTANCE. WB, 1943. *Vincent Sherman.* Sp: John Van Druten & Lenore Coffee, b/o play by John Van Druten. Cast: Miriam Hopkins, Gig Young, John Loder, Dolores Moran, Phillip Reed, Roscoe Karns, Anne Revere, Esther Dale. BD and MH were novelists whose private lives affected one another through the years.

53. MR. SKEFFINGTON. WB, 1944. *Vincent Sherman.* Sp: Philip G. & Julius J. Epstein, b/o novel by "Elizabeth." Cast: Claude Rains, Walter Abel, Richard Waring, George Coulouris, Marjorie Riordan, Robert Shayne, John Alexander, Jerome Cowan, Johnny Mitchell, Dorothy Peterson, Peter Whitney, Halliwell Hobbes. Society belle BD marries financier CR for his money, has his child, separates from him, and grows old trying to retain her youth and beauty.

54. HOLLYWOOD CANTEEN. WB, 1944. *Delmer Daves.* Sp: Delmer Daves. Cast: Joan Leslie, Robert Hutton, Janis Paige, Dane Clark, Richard Erdman. Guest Stars: The Andrews Sisters, Jack Benny, Joe E. Brown, Eddie Cantor, Jack Carson, Joan Crawford, Kitty Carlisle, Helmut Dantine, Faye Emerson, John Garfield, Sydney Greenstreet, Alan Hale, Paul Henreid, Andrea King, Peter Lorre, Ida Lupino, Irene Manning, Joan McCracken, Dolores Moran, Dennis Morgan, Eleanor Parker, William Prince, Joyce Reynolds, Roy Rogers, Alexis Smith, Zachary Scott, Barbara Stanwyck, Craig Stevens, Jane Wyman. As herself, BD described the Canteen's history.

55. THE CORN IS GREEN. WB, 1945. *Irving Rapper.* Sp: Casey Robinson and Frank Cavett, b/o play by Emlyn Williams. Cast: John Dall, Joan Lorring, Nigel Bruce, Rhys Williams, Rosalind Ivan, Mildred Dunnock, Arthur Shields. In a Welsh mining town BD was a schoolmistress who nurtured the genius inside young miner JD.

56. A STOLEN LIFE. WB, 1946. *Curtis Bernhardt.* Sp: Catherine Turney, b/o novel by Karel J. Benes. Cast: Glenn Ford, Dane Clark, Walter Brennan, Charles Ruggles, Bruce Bennett, Peggy Knudsen, Esther Dale, Clara Blandick. BD played twins, one good and the other bad, who love the same man (GF).

57. DECEPTION. WB, 1946. *Irving Rapper.* Sp: John Collier & Joseph Than, b/o play by Louis Verneuil. Cast: Paul Henreid, Claude Rains, John Abbott, Benson Fong, Richard Walsh, Richard Erdman, Russell Arms, Bess Flowers. Concert pianist BD tried to hide her past with CR from new husband PH. A remake of Par's *Jealousy* (1929) with Jeanne Eagels.

58. WINTER MEETING. WB, 1948. *Bretaigne Windust.* Sp: Catherine Turney, b/o novel by Ethel Vance. Cast: James Davis, Janis Paige, John Hoyt, Florence Bates, Walter Baldwin, Ransom Sherman. Spinster poetess BD falls in love with troubled young naval officer.

59. JUNE BRIDE. WB, 1948. *Bretaigne Windust.* Sp: Ranald MacDougall, b/o play by Eileen Tighe & Graeme Lorimer. Cast: Robert Montgomery, Fay Bainter, Betty Lynn, Tom Tully, Barbara Bates, Jerome Cowan, Mary Wickes, James Burke, Raymond Roe, Marjorie Bennett, Ray Montgomery, Debbie Reynolds. Magazine editor BD romanced and fought with RM while preparing a special wedding coverage.

60. BEYOND THE FOREST. WB, 1949. *King Vidor.* Sp: Lenore Coffee, b/o novel by Stuart Engstrand. Cast: Joseph Cotten, David Brian, Ruth Roman, Minor Watson, Dona Drake, Regis Toomey. BD was the bored wife of doctor JC, whose blandness drives her to commit adultery and murder.

61. ALL ABOUT EVE. Fox, 1950. *Joseph L. Mankiewicz.* Sp: Joseph L. Mankiewicz, b/o story by Mary Orr. Cast: Anne

Baxter, George Sanders, Celeste Holm, Gary Merrill, Hugh Marlowe, Thelma Ritter, Marilyn Monroe, Gregory Ratoff, Barbara Bates, Walter Hampden. BD played a famous stage star whose life is changed by unscrupulous AB. BD won the N. Y. Film Critics' Best Actress award. The film won Oscars for Best Picture, Best Supporting Actor (GS), director and screenplay.

62. PAYMENT ON DEMAND. RKO, 1951. *Curtis Bernhardt.* Sp: Bruce Manning & Curtis Bernhardt. Cast: Barry Sullivan, Jane Cowl, Kent Taylor, Betty Lynn, John Sutton, Frances Dee, Peggie Castle, Otto Kruger, Richard Anderson, Natalie Schafer. BD played a middle-aged wife facing divorce. In a flashback sequence BD's daughter, Barbara Merrill, plays her screen daughter.

63. ANOTHER MAN'S POISON. UA, 1952. *Irving Rapper.* Sp: Val Guest, b/o play by Leslie Sands. Cast: Gary Merrill, Emlyn Williams, Anthony Steel, Barbara Murray, Reginald Beckwith, Edna Morris. Mystery writer BD indulged in blackmail and murder to get her secretary's fiance (AS).

64. PHONE CALL FROM A STRANGER. Fox, 1952. *Jean Negulesco.* Sp: Nunnally Johnson, b/o story by I. A. R. Wylie. Cast: Gary Merrill, Shelley Winters, Michael Rennie, Keenan Wynn, Evelyn Varden, Warren Stevens, Beatrice Straight, Craig Stevens, Helen Westcott. BD had the guest-star part of a bedridden invalid. These scenes were later used in a Fox TV drama entitled *Crack-Up* (1955).

65. THE STAR. Fox, 1952. *Stuart Heisler.* Sp: Katherine Albert & Dale Eunson. Cast: Sterling Hayden, Natalie Wood, Warner Anderson, Minor Watson, June Travis, Katherine Warren, Fay Baker, Barbara Lawrence. BD played an Oscar-winning has-been, rescued from jail and the bottle by a former co-star.

66. THE VIRGIN QUEEN. Fox, 1955. (c) *Henry Koster.* Sp: Harry Brown & Mindred Lord. Cast: Richard Todd, Joan Collins, Jay Robinson, Herbert Marshall, Dan O'Herlihy, Robert Douglas, Romney Brent, Rod Taylor. Again BD portrayed Elizabeth I, this time as an older woman.

67. STORM CENTER. Col., 1956.*Daniel Taradash*. Sp: Daniel Taradash & Elick Moll. Cast: Brian Keith, Kim Hunter, Paul Kelly, Kevin Coughlin, Joe Mantell, Kathryn Grant, Edward Platt, Sallie Brophy. Widowed librarian BD lost her job in an effort to keep controversial volumes on her shelves.

68. THE CATERED AFFAIR. MGM, 1956. *Richard Brooks*. Sp: Gore Vidal, b/o teleplay by Paddy Chayefsky. Cast: Ernest Borgnine, Debbie Reynolds, Barry Fitzgerald, Rod Taylor, Robert F. Simon, Madge Kennedy, Dorothy Stickney, Joan Camden, Ray Stricklyn, Dan Tobin, Mae Clarke. BD as Bronx housewife planning her daughter's wedding.

69. JOHN PAUL JONES. WB, 1959. (c) *John Farrow*. Sp: John Farrow & Jesse Lasky, Jr. Cast: Robert Stack, Marisa Pavan, Charles Coburn, Erin O'Brien, Bruce Cabot, Basil Sydney, Thomas Gomez. Guest Stars: Macdonald Carey, Jean Pierre Aumont, David Farrar, Peter Cushing. BD had the cameo role of Catherine the Great.

70. THE SCAPEGOAT. MGM, 1959. *Robert Hamer*. Sp: Gore Vidal & Robert Hamer, b/o novel by Daphne Du Maurier. Cast: Alec Guinness, Nicole Maurey, Irene Worth, Pamela Brown, Annabel Bartlett, Geoffrey Keen, Peter Bull, Alan Webb. AG played the dual role of an English professor and a French count. BD was the count's bedridden mother.

71. POCKETFUL OF MIRACLES. UA, 1961. (c) *Frank Capra*. Sp: Hal Kantor & Harry Tugend, b/o screenplay by Robert Riskin and story by Damon Runyon. Cast: Glenn Ford, Hope Lange, Arthur O'Connell, Peter Falk, Thomas Mitchell, Edward Everett Horton, Mickey Shaughnessy, David Brian, Sheldon Leonard, Ann-Margret, Peter Mann, Barton MacLane, John Litel, Jerome Cowan, Fritz Feld, Ellen Corby, Mike Mazurki. A remake of Capra's 1933 *Lady for a Day,* with BD in the Cinderella role of Apple Annie.

72. WHAT EVER HAPPENED TO BABY JANE? WB, 1961. *Robert Aldrich*. Sp: Lukas Heller, b/o novel by Henry Farrell. Cast: Joan Crawford, Victor Buono, Marjorie Bennett, Maidie

Norman, Anna Lee, Barbara Merrill, Dave Willock. BD and JC played reclusive Hollywood has-beens involved in a bizarre atmosphere of murder and mayhem.

73. DEAD RINGER. WB, 1964. *Paul Henreid.* Sp: Albert Beich & Oscar Millard, b/o story by Rian James. Cast: Karl Malden, Peter Lawford, Philip Carey, Jean Hagen, George Macready, Estelle Winwood, George Chandler, Cyril Delevanti, Monika Henreid. Again BD portrayed twins, one of whom killed the other out of jealousy and vengeance. A remake of Dolores Del Rio's 1946 Mexican film, *La Otra.*

74. LA NOIA (THE EMPTY CANVAS). Emb., 1964. *Damiano Damiani.* Sp: Tonino Guerra, Ugo Liberatore, & Damiano Damiani, b/o novel by Alberto Moravia. Cast: Horst Buchholz, Catherine Spaak, Daniela Rocca, Lea Padovani, Isa Miranda, Georges Wilson. BD was the wealthy American mother of frustrated artist HB.

75. WHERE LOVE HAS GONE. Para., 1964. (c) *Edward Dmytryk.* Sp: John Michael Hayes, b/o novel by Harold Robbins. Cast: Susan Hayward, Michael Connors, Joey Heatherton, Jane Greer, DeForest Kelley, George Macready, Anne Seymour. Wealthy dowager BD meddled in the life of daughter SH, whose lover was killed by *her* daughter (JH).

76. HUSH . . . HUSH, SWEET CHARLOTTE. Fox, 1964. *Robert Aldrich.* Sp: Henry Farrell & Lukas Heller, b/o story by Henry Farrell. Cast: Olivia de Havilland, Joseph Cotten, Agnes Moorehead, Cecil Kellaway, Victor Buono, Mary Astor, William Campbell, Bruce Dern, George Kennedy, Ellen Corby. BD was an aging, demented recluse forced to recall the horrible incidents that made her that way.

77. THE NANNY. Fox, 1965. *Seth Holt.* Sp: Jimmy Sangster, b/o novel by Evelyn Piper. Cast: Wendy Craig, Jill Bennett, James Villiers, William Dix, Pamela Franklin, Jack Watling, Maurice Denham. Kindly family nursemaid BD matched wits with a ten-year-old boy (WD) who accused her of attempted murder.

78. THE ANNIVERSARY. Fox, 1968. (c) *Roy Ward Baker*. Sp: Jimmy Sangster, b/o play by Bill MacIlwraith. Cast: Sheila Hancock, Jack Hedley, James Cossins, Christian Roberts, Elaine Taylor. Ten years after her unlamented husband's death, BD celebrated the occasion with her mother-dominated sons.

79. CONNECTING ROOMS. L.S.D., 1971. (c) *Franklin Gollings*. Sp: Franklin Gollings, b/o play by Marion Hart. Cast: Michael Redgrave, Alexis Kanner, Kay Walsh, Gabrielle Drake, Olga Georges-Picot, Leo Genn, Richard Wyler. Cellist BD took an interest in the problems of fellow-roomer MR.

80. BUNNY O'HARE. AIP, 1971. (c) *Gerd Oswald*. Sp: Stanley Z. Cherry & Coslough Johnson, b/o story by Stanley Z. Cherry. Cast: Ernest Borgnine, Jack Cassidy, Joan Delaney, Jay Robinson, John Astin, Reva Rose. Widow BD joined forces with EB to rob the bank that dispossessed her.

81. MADAME SIN. I.T.C., 1972. (c) *David Greene*. Sp: Barry Orringer & David Greene. Cast: Robert Wagner, Denholm Elliott, Gordon Jackson, Dudley Sutton, Catherine Schell, Paul Maxwell. BD was a criminal mastermind who directed sinister international operations from her castle stronghold in Scotland.

82. THE JUDGE AND JAKE WYLER. Univ.— TV, 1972. *David Lowell Rich*. Sp: Davis Shaw, Richard Levinson & William Link. Cast: Doug McClure, Eric Braeden, Joan Van Ark, Gary Conway, Lou Jacobi, James McEachin, Lisabeth Hush, Kent Smith, Barbara Rhoades. BD played a retired judge who runs a private investigation firm concerned with the murder of an heiress's father.

83. LO SCOPONE SCIENTIFICO (*The Scientific Cardplayer*). C.I.C.; 1972. *Luigi Comencini*. Sp: Rodolfo Sonego. Cast: Alberto Sordi, Silvana Mangano, Joseph Cotten, Domenico Modugno, Mario Carotenuto. BD was an eccentric old American millionairess obsessed with winning at cards on the Continent.

INDEX

(Page numbers italicized indicate photographs)

152

153

154

158

ABOUT THE AUTHOR
Jerry Vermilye is an incurable movie addict whose reviews and articles have appeared in *Films in Review, Film Fan Monthly, Screen Facts, The Independent Film Journal,* and Andy Warhol's *InterView.* He is also the author of *Burt Lancaster,* and is movie-listings editor for *TV Guide.* He lives in Manhattan.

ABOUT THE EDITOR
Ted Sennett has been attending and enjoying movies since the age of two. He has written about films for magazines and newspapers, and is the author of *Warner Brothers Presents,* a survey of the great Warners films of the thirties and forties. A publishing executive, he lives in New Jersey with his wife and three children.